United States Government Accountability Office

GAO

Report to Congressional Requesters

May 2012

CRITICAL INFRASTRUCTURE PROTECTION

DHS Could Better Manage Security Surveys and Vulnerability Assessments

D1301455

GAO

Accountability ★ Integrity ★ Reliability

GAO-12-378

CRITICAL INFRASTRUCTURE PROTECTION

DHS Could Better Manage Security Surveys and Vulnerability Assessments

Highlights of GAO-12-378, a report to congressional requesters

Why GAO Did This Study

Natural disasters, such as Hurricane Katrina, and terrorist attacks, such as the 2005 bombings in London, highlight the importance of protecting CIKR—assets and systems vital to the economy or health of the nation. DHS issued the NIPP in June 2006 (updated in 2009) to provide the approach for integrating the nation's CIKR. Because the private sector owns most of the nation's CIKR—for example, energy production facilities—DHS encourages asset owners and operators to voluntarily participate in surveys or vulnerability assessments of existing security measures at those assets. This includes nationally significant CIKR that DHS designates as high priority. In response to a request, this report assesses the extent to which DHS has (1) taken action to conduct surveys and assessments among high–priority CIKR, (2) shared the results of these surveys and assessments with asset owners or operators, and (3) assessed the effectiveness of surveys and assessments and identified actions taken, if any, to improve them. GAO, among other things, reviewed laws, analyzed data identifying high-priority assets and activities performed from fiscal years 2009 through 2011, and interviewed DHS officials.

What GAO Recommends

GAO recommends that, among other things, DHS develop plans for its efforts to improve the collection and organization of data and the timeliness of survey and assessment results, and gather and act upon additional information from asset owners and operators about why improvements were or were not made. DHS concurred with the recommendations.

View GAO-12-378. For more information, contact Stephen L. Caldwell at (202) 512-8777 or caldwells@gao.gov.

What GAO Found

The Department of Homeland Security (DHS) has conducted about 2,800 security surveys and vulnerability assessments on critical infrastructure and key resources (CIKR). DHS directs its protective security advisors to contact owners and operators of high-priority CIKR to offer to conduct surveys and assessments. However, DHS is not positioned to track the extent to which these are performed at high-priority CIKR because of inconsistencies between the databases used to identify these assets and those used to identify surveys and assessments conducted. GAO compared the two databases and found that of the 2,195 security surveys and 655 vulnerability assessments conducted for fiscal years 2009 through 2011, 135 surveys and 44 assessments matched and another 106 surveys and 23 assessments were potential matches for high-priority facilities. GAO could not match additional high-priority facilities because of inconsistencies in the way data were recorded in the two databases, for example, assets with the same company name had different addresses or an asset at one address had different names. DHS officials acknowledged that the data did not match and have begun to take actions to improve the collection and organization of the data. However, DHS does not have milestones and timelines for completing these efforts consistent with standards for project management. By developing a plan with time frames and milestones consistent with these standards DHS would be better positioned to provide a more complete picture of its progress.

DHS shares the results of security surveys and vulnerability assessments with asset owners or operators but faces challenges doing so. A GAO analysis of DHS data from fiscal year 2011 showed that DHS was late meeting its (1) 30-day time frame—as required by DHS guidance—for delivering the results of its security surveys 60 percent of the time and (2) 60-day time frame—expected by DHS managers for delivering the results of its vulnerability assessments—in 84 percent of the instances. DHS officials acknowledged the late delivery of survey and assessment results and said they are working to improve processes and protocols. However, DHS has not established a plan with time frames and milestones for managing this effort consistent with the standards for project management. Also, the National Infrastructure Protection Plan (NIPP), which emphasizes partnering and voluntary information sharing, states that CIKR partners need to be provided with timely and relevant information that they can use to make decisions. Developing a plan with time frames and milestones for improving timeliness could help DHS provide asset owners and operators with the timely information they need to consider security enhancements.

DHS uses a follow-up tool to assess the results of security surveys and assessments performed at CIKR assets, and are considering upgrades to the tool. However, DHS could better measure results and improve program management by capturing additional information. For example, key information, such as why certain improvements were or were not made by asset owners and operators that have received security surveys, could help DHS improve its efforts. Further, information on barriers to making improvements—such as the cost of security enhancements—could help DHS better understand asset owners and operators' rationale in making decisions and thereby help improve its programs. Taking steps to gather additional information could help keep DHS better informed for making decisions in managing its programs.

_____ United States Government Accountability Office

Contents

Figures

Abbreviations

BZPP	Buffer Zone Protection Plan
CIKR	critical infrastructure and key resources
DHS	Department of Homeland Security
ECIP	Enhanced Critical Infrastructure Protection
HSPD	Homeland Security Presidential Directive
IP	Office of Infrastructure Protection
LENS	Link Encrypted Network System
NAR	National Critical Infrastructure and Key Resources Protection Annual Report
NCIPP	National Critical Infrastructure Prioritization Program
NGB	National Guard Bureau
NIPP	National Infrastructure Protection Plan
NPPD	National Protection and Programs Directorate
PSA	protective security advisor
PSCD	Protective Security Coordination Division
RRAP	Regional Resiliency Assessment Program
SAV	Site Assistance Visit
SCC	sector coordinating council
SSA	sector-specific agency

May 31, 2012

The Honorable Bennie G. Thompson
Ranking Member
Committee on Homeland Security
House of Representatives

The Honorable Sheila Jackson Lee
Ranking Member
Subcommittee on Transportation Security
Committee on Homeland Security
House of Representatives

In 2005, Hurricane Katrina devastated the Gulf Coast, damaging critical infrastructure, such as oil refineries; electric power lines; water mains; and cellular phone towers. More recently, in 2011, a major earthquake and related tsunami devastated eastern Japan, damaging critical infrastructure, such as dams, buildings, and power plants. The damage and resulting chaos disrupted government and business functions alike, producing cascading effects far beyond the physical location of these events. Threats against critical infrastructure are not limited to natural disasters, as demonstrated by the terrorist attacks of September 11, 2001, and the 2005 suicide bombings in London where terrorists disrupted the city's transportation and mobile telecommunication infrastructure. In March 2007, we reported that our nation's critical infrastructures and key resources (CIKR)—assets and systems, whether physical or virtual, so vital to the United States that their incapacity or destruction would have a debilitating impact on national security, national economic security, national public health or safety, or any combination of those matters—continue to be vulnerable to a wide variety of threats.[1] Because the private sector owns the vast majority of the nation's CIKR—banking and financial institutions, commercial facilities, telecommunications networks, and energy production and transmission facilities, among others—it is vital that the public and private sectors work together to protect these assets and systems.

---

[1] GAO, *Critical Infrastructure: Challenges Remain in Protecting Key Sectors*, GAO-07-626T (Washington, D.C.: Mar. 20, 2007).

In 2006, the Department of Homeland Security (DHS) issued the National Infrastructure Protection Plan (NIPP), which provides the overarching approach for integrating the nation's CIKR protection and resilience initiatives into a single national effort.[2] The NIPP sets forth a risk management framework and details the roles and responsibilities for DHS and other federal, state, regional, local, tribal, territorial, and private sector partners implementing the NIPP.[3] The NIPP also outlines the roles and responsibilities of sector-specific agencies (SSA), the various federal departments and agencies that are responsible for CIKR protection and resilience activities in 18 specific CIKR sectors, such as the chemical, commercial facilities, energy, and transportation sectors.[4] The NIPP emphasizes the importance of collaboration and partnering with and among the various partners and voluntary information sharing between the private sector and DHS. Consistent with the NIPP, DHS issues the National Critical Infrastructure and Key Resources Protection Annual Report (NAR) that summarizes risk mitigation and resiliency[5] activities across DHS and the 18 CIKR sectors.[6] Further, as part of its risk management strategy, DHS has established the National Critical Infrastructure Prioritization Program (NCIPP), which uses a tiered approach to identify nationally significant CIKR each year. This high-priority CIKR are categorized as either level 1 or level 2 based on the

[2] DHS, *National Infrastructure Protection Plan* (Washington, D.C.: June 2006). DHS updated the NIPP in January 2009 to include resiliency. See DHS, *National Infrastructure Protection Plan, Partnering to Enhance Protection and Resiliency* (Washington, D.C.: January 2009).

[3] Broadly defined, risk management is a process that helps policymakers assess risk, strategically allocate finite resources, and take actions under conditions of uncertainty.

[4] According to the NIPP, sectors are defined as a logical collection of assets, systems, or networks that provide a common function to the economy, government, or society. The 18 sectors are defined within the context of Homeland Security Presidential Directive 7 (HSPD-7), which directed DHS to establish uniform policies, approaches, guidelines, and methodologies for integrating federal infrastructure protection and risk management activities within and across CIKR sectors. Homeland Security Presidential Directive Number 7 (Washington, D.C.: Dec. 17, 2003). Seventeen sectors were established pursuant to HSPD-7. DHS established an 18th sector—critical manufacturing—pursuant to the directive in 2008. App. I lists the SSAs and their sectors.

[5] According to DHS, resiliency is the ability to resist, absorb, recover from, or successfully adapt to adversity or a change in conditions.

[6] See DHS, *2010 National Critical Infrastructure and Key Resources Protection Annual Report* (July 2010). According to the NIPP, DHS recommends priorities and requirements for CIKR protection to the Executive Office of the President through the NAR.

consequence to the nation in terms of loss of life or economic impact. The levels are used to enhance decision making related to CIKR protection and can include a range of businesses or assets in a local geographic area, such as refineries, water treatment plants, or commercial facilities, as well as the information and data systems that ensure their continued operation. According to DHS, the overwhelming majority of the assets and systems identified as high priority are classified as level 2. Only a small subset of assets meet the level 1 consequence threshold—those whose loss or damage could result in major national or regional impacts similar to the impacts of Hurricane Katrina or the September 11, 2001, attacks.

Within DHS, the Office of Infrastructure Protection (IP) in the National Protection and Programs Directorate (NPPD) is responsible for CIKR protection and resilience. DHS coordinates through SSAs and other sector partners for each of the CIKR sectors to identify security overlaps and gaps as they implement the NIPP framework. While other entities may possess and exercise regulatory authority over CIKR to address security, such as for the chemical, transportation, and nuclear sectors, IP generally relies on voluntary efforts to secure CIKR because of its limited authority to directly regulate most CIKR.[7] The voluntary efforts include the Enhanced Critical Infrastructure Protection (ECIP) security surveys and Site Assistance Visit (SAV) vulnerability assessments DHS conducts at assets across the 18 sectors. ECIP security surveys are voluntary half to full-day surveys DHS conducts to assess overall asset security and increase security awareness, the results of which are presented to CIKR owners and operators in a way that allows them to see how their assets' security measures compare to those of similar assets in the same sector. ECIP security survey results do not provide assets with recommendations or options to enhance protective measures. Participation in SAV vulnerability assessments is also voluntary and these assessments can take up to 3 days to complete. These assessments identify security gaps at assets and are used to provide options to enhance protective

---

[7] Our past work has shown that DHS leverages existing regulatory frameworks, where applicable, to implement the NIPP with its security partners within and across the 18 sectors and identify CIKR security overlaps and gaps to enhance and supplement existing sector regulations. See GAO, *Critical Infrastructure Protection: DHS Has Taken Action Designed to Identify and Address Overlaps and Gaps in Critical Infrastructure Security Activities*, GAO-11-537R (Washington, D.C.: May 19, 2011), and *Critical Infrastructure Protection: DHS Efforts to Assess and Promote Resiliency Are Evolving but Program Management Could Be Strengthened*, GAO-10-772 (Washington, D.C.: Sept. 23, 2010).

measures and resilience to CIKR owners and operators. DHS field representatives, called protective security advisors (PSA), are responsible for working with CIKR owners and operators to conduct these surveys and assessments. As of July 2011, there were 88 PSA positions in various locations throughout the country. DHS shares information on the results of these efforts with various stakeholders, generally on a need-to-know basis.[8]

Given the voluntary nature of DHS's CIKR program, the importance of collaboration and partnering with and among the various partners, and the need to identify and mitigate security and resilience gaps, you asked that we examine DHS efforts to manage and measure the impact of its voluntary security survey and vulnerability assessment programs. Specifically, we assessed the extent to which DHS has

- taken action to conduct security surveys and vulnerability assessments among high-priority CIKR to improve their security postures;

- shared the results of security surveys and vulnerability assessments with asset owners and operators and SSAs; and

- assessed the effectiveness of the security survey and vulnerability assessment programs and identified actions, if any, to improve management of these programs.

To meet our objectives, we reviewed applicable laws, regulations, and directives as well as IP policies and procedures for conducting security surveys and vulnerability assessments, providing their results, and assessing the effectiveness of these programs. We also interviewed IP officials in Washington, D.C., responsible for administering these programs and obtained and assessed IP data on the conduct and management of its security surveys and vulnerability assessments. In so doing, we (1) compared IP data on security surveys and vulnerability assessments conducted for fiscal years 2009 through 2011 with IP lists of high-priority assets over the same period, (2) reviewed IP data on the conduct of security surveys and vulnerability assessments and the delivery of those surveys and assessments to asset owners and

---

[8] Our review focused on IP's voluntary ECIP and SAV programs, which we refer to as security surveys and vulnerability assessments.

GAO-12-378 Critical Infrastructure Protection

operators, and (3) analyzed IP data on its efforts to follow up with asset owners and operators to measure whether they had made changes to enhance the security of their assets as a result of DHS security surveys and vulnerability assessments conducted at their assets for fiscal years 2009 through 2011. We then compared the results of our analyses with various criteria, including DHS policies and procedures outlined in the NIPP;[9] IP guidelines on the conduct and delivery of and follow-up to security surveys and vulnerability assessments; our *Standards for Internal Control in the Federal Government*;[10] and our reports on performance measurement, including those on ways to use program data to measure results.[11] We discussed the sources of the data and IP's quality assurance procedures with agency officials and determined that the data were sufficiently reliable to provide a general overview of the program; limitations are discussed later in this report.

Also, we interviewed SSA officials in Washington, D.C., representing four selected sectors—the water, commercial facilities, energy, and dams sectors—to determine whether these SSAs received the results of security surveys and vulnerability assessments and, if so, how the information was used. We selected these sectors because assets in these sectors underwent numerous vulnerability assessments and security surveys over the period and had a mix of SSA partners. Specifically, DHS was the SSA for two of the sectors—the commercial facilities and dams sectors. The Department of Energy and the

---

[9] DHS, *National Infrastructure Protection Plan, Partnering to Enhance Protection and Resiliency*.

[10] GAO, *Standards for Internal Control in the Federal Government*, GAO/AIMD 00-21.3.1 (Washington, D.C.: November 1999). Internal control is an integral component of an organization's management that provides reasonable assurance that the following objectives are being achieved: effectiveness and efficiency of operations, reliability of financial reporting, and compliance with applicable laws and regulations. These standards, issued pursuant to the requirements of the Federal Managers' Financial Integrity Act of 1982 (FMFIA), provide the overall framework for establishing and maintaining internal control in the federal government. Also pursuant to FMFIA, the Office of Management and Budget issued Circular A-123, revised December 21, 2004, to provide the specific requirements for assessing the reporting on internal controls. Internal control standards and the definition of internal control in Circular A-123 are based on GAO's *Standards for Internal Control in the Federal Government*.

[11] GAO, *Managing For Results: Assessing the Quality of Program Performance Data*, GAO/GGD-00-140R (Washington, D.C.: May 25, 2000), and *Managing for Results: Challenges in Producing Credible Performance Information*, GAO/T-GGD/RCED-00-134 (Washington, D.C.: Mar. 22, 2000).

Environmental Protection Agency were the SSAs for the other two sectors—the energy sector and the water sector, respectively. In addition, we met with owners and operators of 10 high-priority assets in New Jersey, Virginia, and California to obtain their views on DHS efforts to conduct security surveys and vulnerability assessments and provide results. We selected these locations because they contained assets on the high-priority list and had a number of security surveys and vulnerability assessments performed. During our visits to the 10 assets in these locations, we also met with responsible PSAs from our sample states to discuss actions that they take to conduct these surveys and assessments, promote participation among asset owners and operators, provide them the results of security surveys and assessments at their assets, and measure results. The information from our interviews with SSA officials, as well as asset owners and operators and PSAs in the three states, are not generalizable to the universe of CIKR sectors and assets and PSAs throughout the country. However, they provide valuable insights into IP efforts to conduct and manage its security survey and vulnerability assessment programs. With regard to PSAs, we also conducted a survey of 83 of the 88 PSAs nationwide—those with 1 or more years of experience—to obtain their views on various aspects of the security survey and vulnerability assessment programs, including the value of the programs in enhancing CIKR protection and resilience and the challenges PSAs face in promoting and executing the surveys and assessments. We administered our survey from October to November 2011 and received a 96 percent (80 of 83) response rate.

We conducted this performance audit from June 2011 through May 2012 in accordance with generally accepted government auditing standards. Those standards require that we plan and perform the audit to obtain sufficient, appropriate evidence to provide a reasonable basis for our findings and conclusions based on our audit objectives. We believe that the evidence obtained provides a reasonable basis for our findings and conclusions based on our audit objectives. Appendix II discusses our objectives, scope, and methodology and our survey of PSAs in greater detail.

Background

The Homeland Security Act of 2002 created DHS and gave the department wide-ranging responsibilities for, among other things, leading and coordinating the overall national critical infrastructure protection effort.[12] Homeland Security Presidential Directive (HSPD) 7 further defined critical infrastructure protection responsibilities for DHS and SSAs. HSPD-7 directed DHS to establish uniform policies, approaches, guidelines, and methodologies for integrating federal infrastructure protection and risk management activities within and across CIKR sectors. Various other statutes and directives provide specific legal authorities for both cross sector and sector-specific protection and resiliency programs. For example, the Public Health Security and Bioterrorism Preparedness and Response Act of 2002 was enacted to improve the ability of the United States to prevent, prepare for, and respond to acts of bioterrorism and other public health emergencies, and the Pandemic and All-Hazards Preparedness Act of 2006 addresses, among other things, public health security and all-hazards preparedness and response.[13] Also, the Cyber Security Research and Development Act, enacted in January 2002, authorized funding through fiscal year 2007for the National Institute of Standards and Technology and the National Science Foundation to facilitate increased research and development for computer and network security and to support related research fellowships and training.[14] CIKR protection issues are also covered under various presidential directives, including HSPD-5 and HSPD-8. HSPD-5 calls for coordination among all levels of government as well as between the government and the private sector for managing domestic incidents, and HSPD-8 establishes policies to strengthen national preparedness to prevent, detect, respond to, and recover from threatened or actual domestic terrorist attacks, major disasters, and other

---

[12] See generally Pub. L. No. 107-296, 116 Stat. 2135 (2002). Title II of the Homeland Security Act, as amended, primarily addresses the department's responsibilities for critical infrastructure protection.

[13] See generally Pub. L. No. 107-188, 116 Stat. 594 (2002); Pub. L. No. 109-417, 120 Stat. 2831 (2006).

[14] See generally Pub. L. No. 107-305, 116 Stat. 2367 (2002). Other statutes referenced in the NIPP as providing specific legal authorities for both cross sector and sector-specific protection and resiliency programs include, generally, the Implementing Recommendations of the 9/11 Commission Act of 2007, Pub. L. No. 110-53, 121 Stat. 266; the Federal Information Security Management Act, Pub. L. No. 107-347, tit. III, 116 Stat. 2899, 2946-61 (codified in part, as amended, at 44 U.S.C. §§ 3541-49); the Critical Infrastructure Information Act of 2002, Pub. L. No. 107-296, tit. II, subtit. B, 116 Stat. at 2150-55 (codified at 6 U.S.C. §§ 131-34); the Maritime Transportation Security Act of 2002, Pub. L. No. 107-295, 116 Stat. 2064; the Aviation and Transportation Security Act, Pub. L. No. 107-71, 115 Stat. 597 (2001); and the Energy Policy and Conservation Act, Pub. L. No. 94-163, 89 Stat. 871 (1975).

emergencies.[15] According to the NIPP, these separate authorities and directives are tied together as part of the national approach for CIKR protection through the unifying framework established in HSPD-7.

NPPD's IP is responsible for working with public and private sector CIKR partners in the 18 sectors and leads the coordinated national effort to mitigate risk to the nation's CIKR through the development and implementation of CIKR protection and resilience programs. Using a sector partnership model, IP's Partnership and Outreach Division works with sector representatives, including asset owners and operators, to develop, facilitate, and sustain strategic relationships and information sharing. IP's Protective Security Coordination Division (PSCD) provides programs and initiatives to enhance CIKR protection and resilience and reduce risk associated with all-hazards incidents. In so doing, PSCD works with CIKR owners and operators and state and local responders to (1) assess vulnerabilities, interdependencies, capabilities, and incident consequences; (2) develop, implement, and provide national coordination for protective programs; and (3) facilitate CIKR response to and recovery from incidents. Related to these efforts, PSCD has deployed the aforementioned PSAs in 50 states and Puerto Rico, with deployment locations based on population density and major concentrations of CIKR. In these locations, PSAs are to act as the link between state, local, tribal, and territorial organizations and DHS infrastructure mission partners and are to

- assist with ongoing state and local CIKR security efforts by establishing and maintaining relationships with state, local, tribal, territorial, and private sector organizations;
- support the development of the national risk picture by conducting vulnerability and security assessments to identify security gaps and potential vulnerabilities in the nation's most critical infrastructures; and

---

[15] Other CIKR-related presidential directives include HSPD-3, which addresses implementation of the Homeland Security Advisory System; HSPD-9, which establishes a national policy to defend the nation's agriculture and food system; HSPD-10, which addresses U.S. efforts to prevent, protect against, and mitigate biological weapons attacks perpetrated against the United States and its global interests; HSPD-19, which addresses the prevention and detection of, protection against, and response to terrorist use of explosives in the United States; HSPD-20, which addresses the establishment of a comprehensive and effective national continuity policy; and HSPD-22, which, as described in the NIPP, addresses the ability of the United States to prevent, protect, respond to, and recover from terrorist attacks employing toxic chemicals.

• share vulnerability information and protective measure suggestions with local partners and asset owners and operators.

Enhanced Critical Infrastructure Protection Security Surveys

As part of their ongoing activities, PSAs are responsible for promoting the ECIP Initiative. Launched in September 2007, the ECIP Initiative is a voluntary program focused on forming or maintaining partnerships between DHS and CIKR owners and operators of high-priority level 1 and level 2 assets and systems, as well as other assets of significant value. According to DHS guidance, PSAs are to schedule ECIP visits with owners and operators in their districts using lists of high-priority and other significant assets provided by PSCD each year, with visits to level 1 assets being the first priority, and visits to level 2 assets being the second priority. Visits to other significant assets are to receive subsequent priority based on various factors, including whether they are of significant value based on the direction of IP; have been identified by the state homeland security office; or represent a critical dependency associated with higher-priority assets already identified. If an asset owner or operator agrees to participate in an ECIP visit, PSAs are to meet with the owner or operator to assess overall site security, identify gaps, provide education on security, and promote communication and information sharing among asset owners and operators, DHS, and state governments.[16]

One of the components of the ECIP Initiative is the security survey, formally called the Infrastructure Survey Tool, which a PSA can use to gather information on the asset's current security posture and overall security awareness. If the asset owner or operator agrees to participate in the security survey, the PSA works with the owner or operator to apply the survey, which assesses more than 1,500 variables covering six major components—information sharing, security management, security force, protective measures, physical security, or dependencies—as well as 42 more specific subcomponents within those categories. For example, within the category "physical security" possible subcomponents include fences, gates, parking, lighting, and access control, among others. Once the survey is complete, the PSA submits the data to Argonne National Laboratory, which analyzes the data to produce protective measures index scores ranging from 0 (low protection) to 100 (high protection) for

---

[16] According to DHS guidelines, SSAs are to be invited to attend the ECIP and can attend if the asset owner and operator agree that SSA officials can attend.

the entire asset and for each component of the survey. Argonne National Laboratory also uses the data to produce a "dashboard"—an interactive graphic tool that is provided to the asset owner or operator by the PSA. The dashboard displays the asset's overall protective measures score, the score for each of the six major components, the mean protective measures score and major component scores for all like assets in the sector or subsector that have undergone a security survey, and high and low scores recorded for each component for all sector or subsector assets that have undergone a security survey. The asset score and the scores for other like assets show the asset owner or operator how the asset compares to similar assets in the sector. The asset owner can also use the dashboard to see the effect of making security upgrades to its asset. For example, if the dashboard shows a low score for physical security relative to those of other like assets, the owner or operator can add data on perimeter fencing to see how adding or improving a fence would increase the asset's score, thereby bringing it more in line with those of other like assets. Figure 1 provides an example of the dashboard produced as a result of the security survey.

Figure 1: Illustration of Protective Measure Index Dashboard Provided to Asset Owners and Operators Following a Security Survey

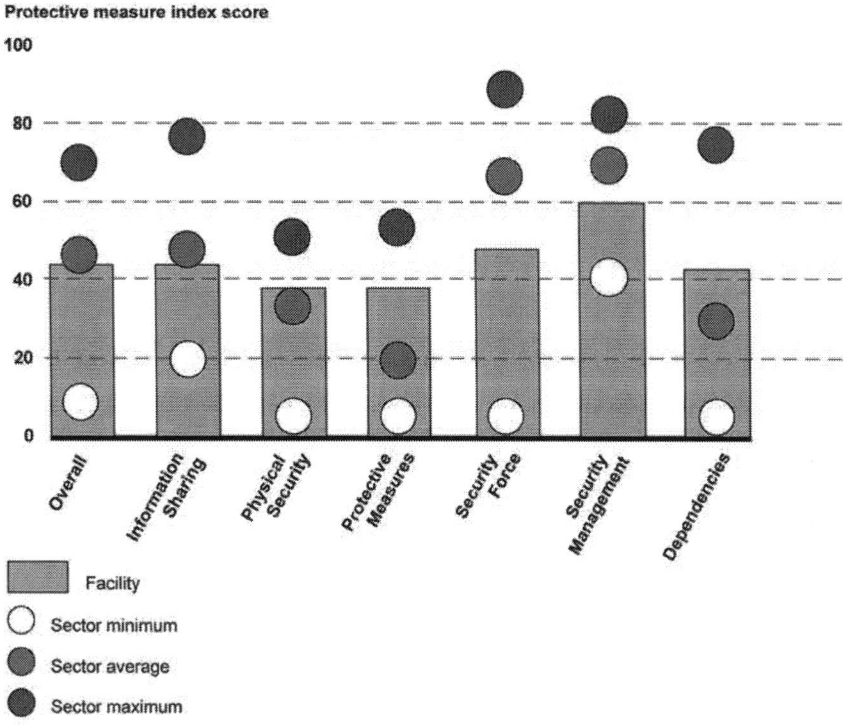

Protective measure index score

- Facility
- Sector minimum
- Sector average
- Sector maximum

Source: Office of Infrastructure Protection, DHS.

Related to these security surveys, DHS also produced, from calendar years 2009 through 2011, summaries of the results of the security surveys related to sector or subsector security postures, known as sector summaries. These sector summaries were provided directly to SSAs in 2009 and 2010, and according to program officials were made available to SSAs in 2011 for sectors upon request. Unlike the summaries in past years, the 2011 summaries also included an "options for consideration" section that identified specific protective measures that had been adopted by the top 20 percent of assets in the sector or subsector as measured by the overall protective measures score.

Site Assistance Visit Vulnerability Assessments

DHS also uses vulnerability assessments to identify security gaps and provide options for consideration to mitigate these identified gaps. These assessments are generally on-site, asset-specific assessments conducted at the request of asset owners and operators. As of September 30, 2011, DHS had conducted more than 1,500 vulnerability assessments. Generally, vulnerability assessments are conducted at individual assets by IP assessment teams in coordination with PSAs, SSAs, state and local government organizations (including law enforcement and emergency management officials), asset owners and operators, and the National Guard, which is engaged as part of a joint initiative between DHS and the National Guard Bureau (NGB). These assessment teams are staffed via an interagency agreement between DHS and NGB and include two national guardsmen—a physical security planner and a systems analyst, one of whom serves as the team lead. They may also be supplemented by contractor support or other federal personnel, such as PSAs or subject matter experts, when requested. Argonne National Laboratory staff then finalize the vulnerability assessment report—which includes options for consideration to increase an asset's ability to detect and prevent terrorist attacks and mitigation options that address the identified vulnerabilities of the asset—and provide it to the PSA for delivery. The asset owners and operators that volunteer for the vulnerability assessments are the primary recipients of the analysis. The vulnerability assessment is developed using a questionnaire that focuses on various aspects of the security of an asset, such as vulnerabilities associated with access to asset air handling systems, physical security, and the ability to deter or withstand a blast or explosion. The vulnerability assessment report also contains a section called "options for consideration" where DHS makes suggestions to improve asset security or reduce identified vulnerabilities. For example, one vulnerability assessment report made suggestions to the asset owners or operators to explore the option of installing additional cameras to improve video surveillance in certain locations, install additional barriers to prevent vehicles from entering the facility at high speeds, and increase the training of its security staff.

DHS revised the vulnerability assessment methodology in 2010 to enhance the analytical capabilities of IP. According to DHS officials, vulnerability assessments developed prior to 2010 did not have a consistent approach for gathering data on assets and did not produce results that were comparable from asset to asset. They also did not incorporate an approach for assessing asset resilience. DHS reported that the revised vulnerability assessment is intended to incorporate about 75 percent of the questions currently asked during an ECIP security survey, including questions on resilience, to bring the tool more in line with the security survey. As a result, vulnerability assessments completed beginning in 2011 have the capability to produce a dashboard similar to that produced from security surveys. By revising the assessment methodology, DHS intends to ensure that the data collected during the vulnerability assessment can be compared within and across sectors and subsectors while still providing each asset an assessment specific to that asset, including options for consideration to reduce vulnerability.

Regional Resiliency Assessment Program

While not the focus of this review, DHS has developed the Regional Resiliency Assessment Program (RRAP) to assess vulnerability and risk associated with resiliency. The RRAP is an analysis of infrastructure "clusters," regions, and systems in major metropolitan areas that uses security surveys and vulnerability assessments, along with other tools, in its analysis. The RRAP evaluates CIKR on a regional level to examine vulnerabilities, threats, and potential consequences from an all-hazards perspective to identify dependencies, interdependencies, cascading effects, resiliency characteristics, and gaps. The RRAP assessments are conducted by DHS officials, including PSAs in collaboration with SSAs; other federal officials; state, local, territorial, and tribal officials; and the private sector depending upon the sectors and assets selected as well as a resiliency subject matter expert(s). The results of the RRAP are to be used to enhance the overall security posture of the assets, surrounding communities, and the geographic region covered by the project and is shared with the state.[17] According to DHS officials, the results of specific asset-level assessments conducted as part of the RRAP are made available to asset owners and operators and other partners (as appropriate), but the final analysis and report are delivered to the state where the RRAP occurred. Further, according to DHS, while it continues to perform surveys and assessments at individual assets, prioritizing efforts to focus on regional assessments allows DHS to continue to meet evolving threats and challenges.

---

[17] In doing the RRAP, DHS does a comprehensive analysis of a region's CIKR and protection and prevention capabilities and focuses on (1) integrating vulnerability and capability assessments and infrastructure protection planning efforts; (2) identifying security gaps and corresponding options for consideration to improve prevention, protection, and resiliency; (3) analyzing system recovery capabilities and providing options to secure operability during long-term recovery; and (4) assessing state and regional resiliency, mutual aid, coordination, and interoperable communication capabilities.

DHS Faces Challenges Managing Its Efforts to Conduct Security Surveys and Vulnerability Assessments on High-Priority Assets

DHS conducted about 2,800 security surveys and vulnerability assessments during fiscal years 2009 through 2011. In so doing, DHS directed PSAs to contact owners and operators of high-priority assets to offer to conduct voluntary security surveys and vulnerability assessments at their assets and PSAs used these as part of their outreach efforts among these assets. However, DHS faces challenges tracking whether security surveys and vulnerability assessments have been performed at high-priority assets. Furthermore, DHS has not developed institutional performance goals that can be used to measure the extent to which owners and operators of high-priority assets participate in security surveys and vulnerability assessments. In addition, DHS is not positioned to assess why some high-priority asset owners and operators decline to participate in these voluntary surveys and assessments so that it can develop strategies for increasing participation.

Inconsistent Data Make It Challenging to Match Security Surveys and Vulnerability Assessments with High-Priority Assets

DHS is not positioned to track the extent to which it is conducting security surveys and vulnerability assessments on high-priority assets because of inconsistencies between the databases used to identify high-priority assets and to identify surveys and assessments completed. Consistent with the NIPP, DHS prioritizes the participation of high-priority assets in its voluntary security survey and vulnerability assessment programs and uses the NCIPP list of high-priority assets to guide its efforts.[18] In February 2011, DHS issued guidance to PSAs that called for them to form partnerships with owners and operators of high-priority assets in their areas. Under the guidelines, PSAs are to use NCIPP lists of high-priority assets to identify and contact owners and operators of the these assets in their areas that could benefit from participation in the security surveys, for the purpose of reducing potential security vulnerabilities and identifying protective measures in place.[19] PSAs are to conduct outreach directly by meeting with the asset owners and operators to provide information about DHS efforts to improve protection and resiliency,

---

[18] To meet its responsibilities under the Homeland Security Act and HSPD-7, DHS's Homeland Infrastructure Threat and Risk Analysis Center, in cooperation with the PSAs, SSAs, and other CIKR partners, conducts an annual data call to state and federal partners, to build from and update existing high-priority infrastructure inventories as part of the NCIPP.

[19] According to DHS officials, PSAs have conducted 2,946 outreach visits to asset owners and operators during fiscal years 2009 through 2011, of which 1,050 were to high-priority facilities.

sharing information about how an asset owner or operator can request a vulnerability assessment, and offering to conduct a security survey.[20] If the owner or operator agrees to a visit from the PSA, the PSA is to record the date of the visit, and if the owner or operator agrees to participate in a security survey or vulnerability assessment, the PSA is likewise to record the day the security survey or vulnerability assessment was conducted. DHS analysts are then required to record the data provided by the PSAs in DHS's Link Encrypted Network System (LENS) database—DHS's primary database for tracking efforts to promote and complete security surveys and annual assessments.[21] According to DHS guidelines, these data are subject to weekly reviews to ensure that data recorded in LENS are accurate, consistent, and complete. Thus, data on each individual asset should be recorded so that asset sector, name, and physical address reflect a single asset in a specified location throughout the database. For example, according to the guidelines, asset names recorded in LENS should not be recorded with stray asterisks, other special characters, and notes, and to the extent possible, address fields, such as "St" should be captured as "Street."[22]

To determine how many of these activities have been conducted on high-priority assets, we used an automated statistical software program to compare data on security surveys and vulnerability assessments completed in DHS's LENS database with data on high-priority assets on the NCIPP lists for fiscal years 2009 through 2011—the lists PSAs are to use to contact officials representing high-priority assets in their areas.[23] Out of 2,195 security surveys and 655 vulnerability assessments conducted during fiscal years 2009 through 2011, we identified a total of 135 surveys and 44 vulnerability assessments that matched assets on the NCIPP lists of high-priority assets. We also identified an additional 106

---

[20] Our survey of PSAs confirmed that all 80 PSA respondents had received the security survey guidance and associated training, of whom 41 percent (33 of 80) found the guidance very useful for promoting security surveys and 43 percent (34 of 80) found it moderately useful. See app. III for more results from our survey.

[21] The LENS portal is restricted and allows authorized users to obtain, post, and exchange information and access common resources, particularly critical infrastructure information, including security survey data.

[22] A data field is a location in a data set where the same information (such as asset name) is entered for each case.

[23] See app. II for details of our automated process for matching the data.

security surveys and 23 vulnerability assessments that were potential matches with assets on the NCIPP lists of priority assets, but we could not be certain that the assets were the same because of inconsistencies in the way the data were recorded in the two different databases. For example, we found instances where assets that appeared to be the same company or organization were listed in different sectors. We also encountered instances where names of companies at the same address did not match exactly or where companies with the same names had slightly different addresses in the two databases. For example, an asset at 12345 Main Street in Anytown, USA, might appear as ABC Company on one list and ABC on another. Conversely, we also found instances where company names appeared to be the same or similar on both lists, but they were listed at different street addresses or on different streets. In this case, for example, ABC Company might appear as being located on Main Street on one list, and E. Main St. on another.[24]

We contacted DHS officials responsible for maintaining the LENS database and the NCIPP list and told them that we had encountered difficulty matching company names and addresses in the two lists. We explained that our results depended on an asset being described in a similar manner—same name, same address, same sector—in both the NCIPP and LENS databases. These officials acknowledged that the two databases do not match and explained that they have had to match the data manually because of the inconsistencies. Specifically, DHS reported that it reviewed over 10,000 records—including records of security surveys, vulnerability assessments, and the NCIPP lists for fiscal years 2009 through 2011—and manually matched assets that had participated in surveys or assessments with the NCIPP lists of high-priority assets using DHS officials' knowledge of the assets. Based on its efforts, DHS analysts provided a table that showed that DHS conducted 2,128 security surveys and 652 vulnerability assessments, of which it identified 674 surveys and 173 assessments that were conducted on high-priority assets. Thus, by manually matching assets across the two lists, DHS was able to show that the percentage of high-priority assets surveyed and assessed increased significantly. Table 1 illustrates the results of our efforts to match the data using an automated software program and the results of DHS's efforts to manually match the data.

---

[24] The examples provided are intended to illustrate instances where we could not match the two lists with certainty.

GAO-12-378 Critical Infrastructure Protection

Table 1: Comparison of GAO Automated and DHS Manual Matching of Security Surveys and Vulnerability Assessments Conducted on High-Priority Assets during Fiscal Years 2009 through 2011

	Security surveys		Vulnerability assessments	
	GAO	DHS	GAO	DHS
Total activities identified	2,195	2,128	655	652
Activities conducted on high-priority assets	241	674	67	173
Activities conducted on high-priority assets (percentages)	11.0	31.6	10.2	26.5

Sources: GAO analysis of data provided by DHS and DHS analysis of DHS data.

Note: GAO reported activities include the sum of exact and potential matches of activities (security surveys or vulnerability assessments) with the NCIPP lists of high-priority assets. As noted earlier, no other types of DHS assessments are included in this analysis.

DHS officials noted that beginning with the fiscal year 2012 NCIPP lists, they have begun to apply unique numerical identifiers to each asset listed in LENS and the NCIPP lists. According to these officials, once a match is made, the application of unique identifiers to the same assets in both databases is intended to remove uncertainty about which asset is which, regardless of variations in the name or address of the asset. Related to this, DHS officials also said that they have initiated a quality assurance process whereby they use descriptive data—such as geographic coordinates (longitude and latitude)—to verify street addresses and names, thereby giving IP the ability to more readily make matches in those instances where it may have previously experienced difficulty doing so. Nonetheless, they said that the NCIPP list continues to present matching challenges because there have been "significant" changes in the NCIPP list from year to year, but they anticipate fewer changes in the future. Most recently, the format and the organization of the list has changed to focus on clusters—groups of related assets that can be disrupted through a single natural or man-made hazard, excluding the use of weapons of mass destruction—rather than on individual assets. Thus, some assets previously considered high priority as stand-alone assets are now listed as part of a system or as clusters that in and of themselves are no longer considered high priority. According to DHS officials, the introduction of clusters has resulted in other data matching challenges, including the duplicate entry of an NCIPP asset that spans two states; multiple entries for a single asset that is listed both individually and in relation to a cluster or a system, and multiple entries for a single asset within several clusters or systems. DHS officials added that with the assignment of the unique identifier, they expect to be better positioned to cross-reference their program activities with the NCIPP list.

DHS officials have stated that the discrepancies between our analyses and the analysis performed by IP, as well as the confusion created by factors such as changing data sets, made it clear that improvements should be made in the collection and organization of the data. Accordingly, DHS officials said that they are continuing to work with various partners within DHS and its contractors to streamline and better organize the list of high-priority assets and data associated with assessments, surveys, and other IP field activities. However, DHS did not provide milestones and time frames for completing these efforts. DHS appears to be heading in the right direction in taking actions to resolve many of the issues we identified with regard to matching data and data inconsistencies. However, moving forward, DHS would be better positioned if it were to develop milestones and time frames for its plans to accomplish these tasks. Standard practices for project management state that managing a project involves, among other things, developing a timeline with milestone dates to identify points throughout the project to reassess efforts under way to determine whether project changes are necessary.[25] By developing time frames and milestones for streamlining and organizing the lists of high-priority assets and data associated with surveys, assessments, and field activities, DHS would be better positioned to provide a more complete picture of its approach for developing and completing these tasks. It also would provide DHS managers and other decision makers with insights into (1) IP's overall progress in completing these tasks and (2) a basis for determining what, if any, additional actions need to be taken.

DHS's Efforts to Measure Progress Could Be Enhanced with Realistic Institutional Goals

As DHS moves forward to improve its efforts to track the hundreds of security surveys and vulnerability assessments it performs each year, DHS could also better position itself to measure its progress in conducting these surveys and assessments at high-priority assets. We have previously reported that to efficiently and effectively operate, manage, and oversee programs and activities, agencies need reliable information during their planning efforts to set realistic goals and later, as programs are being implemented, to gauge their progress toward achieving those

---

[25] According to the Project Management Institute, *The Standard for Program Management*© (2006), a "road map" provides direction on how a program will be managed and defines its key variables.

goals.[26] In July 2011, the PSCD Deputy Director told us that PSCD had a goal that 50 percent of the security surveys and vulnerability assessments conducted each year be on high-priority assets.[27] However, this goal was not documented; PSCD did not have written goals and the results to date indicate that this goal was not realistic.[28] Specifically, according to DHS's 2010 NAR, less than 40 percent (299 of 763) of security surveys were conducted on high-priority assets from May 1, 2009, through April 30, 2010. For the same time period, DHS's NAR reported that about 33 percent (69 of 212) of vulnerability assessments were conducted on high-priority assets.[29] Setting institutional realistic goals for the number of security surveys and vulnerability assessments conducted at high-priority assets—consistent with DHS's efforts to improve its data on these assets—would enable DHS to better measure its performance and assess the state of security and resiliency at high-priority facilities, across the 18 sectors, over time. For example, if there is a high-priority list consisting of 2,000 facilities, a DHS goal of 500 security surveys and vulnerability assessments conducted on high-priority facilities annually would allow for the potential assessment of all high-priority facilities over a defined period of time. Therefore, DHS could be in a better position to

---

[26] GAO/T-GGD/RCED-00-134.

[27] According to the DHS official responsible for the program, the remaining 50 percent of surveys and assessments are to be performed at assets identified by state and local CIKR partners.

[28] The *Department of Homeland Security Office of Infrastructure Protection Fiscal Year 2008 – 2013 Strategic Plan*, August 2007, identified a goal of completing more than 300 assessments annually by fiscal year 2009. This goal includes vulnerability and other assessments, such as those of the Buffer Zone Protection Plan (BZPP). The BZPP was a DHS-administered grant program designed to help local law enforcement and owners and operators of CIKR increase security in the "buffer zone"—the area outside of a facility that can be used by an adversary to conduct surveillance or launch an attack. According to DHS officials, the BZPP activities included in that goal are no longer conducted. We did not include the BZPP in our analysis because, as noted earlier, we limited the scope of our engagement to the security survey and vulnerability assessment (site assistance visit) activities.

[29] For the NAR reporting period, we identified 41 surveys and 15 vulnerability assessments that matched assets on the NCIPP list. We also identified 41 surveys and 7 vulnerability assessments that were potential matches with assets on the NCIPP list. IP officials provided us with the data used in the NAR so that we could verify that the data reported reflected the actual number of surveys and assessments conducted among high-priority assets; however, consistent with the data-matching efforts described earlier, DHS analysts manually matched their survey and assessment records with the NCIPP lists to generate the NAR data.

identify security strengths and weaknesses at high-priority facilities and within and across sectors and target areas for improvement.[30]

Related to goals and performance measures, DHS officials told us that various factors can affect the number of security surveys and vulnerability assessments conducted at high-priority assets. First, senior IP officials emphasized the distinctly voluntary nature of participation in these programs and said that while they believe these voluntary programs have been very successful, they are just one tool used to establish new or enhance existing relationships with the owners and operators of high-priority assets.[31] Second, DHS officials pointed out that successful outreach to asset owners and operators does not necessarily require that a security survey or vulnerability assessment be conducted. Third, according to DHS officials, they do not want to promote security survey and vulnerability assessment programs too forcefully out of concern that the relationship with an asset owner or operator could be damaged or may not develop.[32] Fourth, they pointed out that some high-priority assets are subject to regulation by separate federal entities, which can limit IP's ability to conduct security surveys and vulnerability assessments. Regarding the latter, our past work has shown that there are some sectors that are subject to specific security laws and regulations, such as the chemical, transportation, and nuclear sectors.[33] In these instances,

---

[30] According to DHS officials, it is expected that the composition of the high-priority list will stabilize because they are now using consequence-based criteria.

[31] Consistent with HSPD-7, DHS pursues a voluntary approach to critical infrastructure protection and coordination.

[32] For example, in addition to outreach to individual asset owners and operators, PSAs are directed to share information on protection and resiliency and promote participation in security surveys and vulnerability assessments to other CIKR stakeholders, including sector- or subsector-specific industry associations, such as the Hotel Security Association.

[33] See GAO-11-537R. For example, the Chemical Facilities Anti-Terrorism Standards (CFATS), promulgated by DHS pursuant to the Department of Homeland Security Appropriations Act, 2007, Pub. L. No. 109-295, § 550, 120 Stat. 1355, 1388-89 (2006), impose requirements on high-risk chemical facilities in the United States to enhance the nation's security by lowering the risk posed by those chemical facilities. See 67 Fed. Reg. 17,688 (Apr. 9, 2007) (codified as amended at 6 C.F.R. pt. 27). Consistent with the fiscal year 2007 DHS appropriations act, CFATS do not apply to facilities regulated pursuant to the Maritime Transportation Security Act of 2002, facilities owned or operated by the Departments of Defense or Energy, facilities subject to regulation by the Nuclear Regulatory Commission, and federally regulated public water systems and water treatment facilities.

DHS officials told us that many of these assets do not receive voluntary surveys and assessments conducted by PSCD. Rather, as we previously reported, PSCD staff told us that they work with the responsible federal entity, such as the U.S. Coast Guard and the Nuclear Regulatory Commission, to identify and address vulnerabilities. Finally, according to the PSCD Deputy Director, shifting priorities based on terrorist threat information, budget constraints, and other department wide priorities, affect the prioritization and distribution of assets participating in these voluntary programs. For example, DHS officials stated that given DHS is placing increased emphasis on regional activities, such as RRAPs, voluntary surveys and assessments are not necessarily focused on individual high-priority assets. They said that expanded focus on regional activities enables IP to meet evolving threats and challenges, but in a budget constrained environment, forces them to prioritize activities so that they can leverage existing resources.[34]

We recognize that various factors can influence whether asset owners and operators participate in DHS's security surveys and assessments, and in some cases, these factors may pose barriers to convincing asset owners and operators to participate. However, as DHS addresses inconsistencies in its data, using those data to establish institutional goals for appropriate levels of voluntary participation could better position DHS to measure how well it is achieving those goals consistent with *Standards for Internal Control in the Federal Government*.[35] Such standards call for agencies to compare actual performance to planned or expected results and analyze significant differences. By being able to identify differences, DHS could develop strategies for overcoming differences or, if necessary, adjust its goals to more realistically reflect the challenges, if any, it faces. Furthermore, according to the NIPP, the use of performance measures—including establishing goals and objectives with specific outcomes or performance targets—is a critical step in the NIPP risk management

---

[34] DHS provided budget figures for the Vulnerability Assessment Branch responsible for SAVs and budget figures for the PSA program that conducts security surveys. These figures indicate that the budget for the Vulnerability Assessment Project could decline from $19.2 million in fiscal year 2012 to a requested $18.5 million in fiscal year 2013.

[35] See GAO/AIMD-00-21.3.1. *Standards for Internal Control in the Federal Government* also calls for accurate and timely recording of information and periodic record reviews to help reduce the risk of errors. DHS officials told us that they conduct data quality checks and DHS guidelines direct such actions. However, the extent to which data were inconsistent indicates that information was not always accurately captured.

process to enable DHS to objectively and quantitatively assess improvement in CIKR protection and resiliency. Specifically, the NIPP states that performance metrics allow NIPP partners to track progress against these priorities and provide a basis for DHS to establish accountability, document actual performance, promote effective management, and provide a feedback mechanism to decision makers. Consistent with the NIPP risk management framework, our past work has shown that leading organizations strive to align their activities to achieve mission-related goals.[36] By using LENS and NCIPP data to establish performance goals, DHS could also be better positioned to identify gaps between expected and actual participation, track progress in achieving higher levels of participation, and ultimately gauge the extent to which protection and resiliency are enhanced for the nation's most critical assets. Relying on institutional goals rather than informal goals would also provide assurance that DHS has a common framework for measuring performance in the face of organizational or personnel changes over time.

DHS Tracks Whether Owners and Operators Decline Surveys and Assessments but Does Not Track Reasons Why They Decline

DHS guidelines issued in February 2011 call for PSAs to document the names and addresses of CIKR asset owners or operators that decline to participate in security survey outreach activities as well as the reasons they declined. DHS officials told us that currently they track aggregate data on declinations but they do not document the reasons why asset owners and operators decline to participate in the security survey and vulnerability assessment programs. In November 2011, DHS provided a list of 69 asset owners or operators that PSAs recorded as having declined to participate in the security surveys from March 2009 through 2011, but these records did not identify reasons for the declinations. Program officials told us that the tool with which they collect declination information is not designed to capture such information. The Deputy Director for PSCD said that in 2012, DHS is developing a survey tool that PSAs can use to record why asset owners or operators decline to participate. Nonetheless, DHS could not provide specifics as to what would be included in the tool, which office would be responsible for implementing it, or time frames for its implementation. Rather, officials told us that they intend to use the results of our review to inform

---

[36] GAO, *Executive Guide: Effectively Implementing the Government Performance and Results Act*, GAO/GGD-96-118 (Washington, D.C.: June 1996).

improvements to the process. Regarding vulnerability assessments, the assessment guidance is silent on whether PSAs are to discuss declinations with asset owners and operators and why they declined. However, PSCD issued guidance in January 2012 that states that the vulnerability assessment guidance is designed to complement the ECIP guidance issued in February 2011.

In our survey of PSAs, PSA respondents provided some anecdotal reasons as to why asset owners and operators may decline to participate. For example, when asked how often they had heard various responses from asset owners and operators that declined to participate in security surveys or vulnerability assessments, PSAs responded that reasons for declinations can include (1) the asset was already subject to federal or state regulation or inspections, (2) the identification of security gaps could render the owner of the asset liable for damages should an incident occur, or (3) assets owner or operator had concerns that the information it provides will not be properly safeguarded by DHS.[37] Figure 2 shows the frequencies of PSA responses of either "often" or "sometimes" to our survey question about the various reasons for declinations that they have heard. Appendix III shows the results of our survey in greater detail.

---

[37] Pursuant to the Critical Infrastructure Information (CII) Act of 2002, DHS established the Protected Critical Infrastructure Information (PCII) program to institute a means to facilitate the voluntary sharing of certain private sector, state, and local CIKR information with the federal government while providing assurances of limited public disclosure under the Freedom of Information Act (5 U.S.C. § 552) and other laws, rules, and processes and that information shared will be properly safeguarded. See 6 U.S.C. §§ 131-34; see also 6 C.F.R. pt. 29 (implementing the CII Act through the establishment of uniform procedures for the receipt, care, and storage of voluntarily submitted CII). DHS has established a PCII program office, which, among other things, is responsible for validating information provided by CIKR partners as PCII and developing protocols to access and safeguard information that is deemed PCII. In June 2011, the DHS Office of Inspector General (OIG) issued a report entitled *Planning, Management, and Systems Issues Hinder DHS' Efforts to Protect Cyberspace and the Nation's Cyber Infrastructure* (OIG-11-89, (Washington, D.C.: June 2011), wherein the OIG did not identify any high-risk system security vulnerabilities associated with the database that houses PCII data. However, the OIG stated that critical infrastructure data may be at risk because of insufficient training and system vulnerabilities. Among other things, the OIG recommended that IP develop a process to track individuals who have access to PCII data and periodically review whether they still needed access and have completed required PCII refresher training. The OIG reported that, in response to this recommendation, NPPD has since begun to track whether individuals who need access to PCII have completed required refresher training, but did not address whether NPPD will implement a process to periodically review whether individuals still need access.

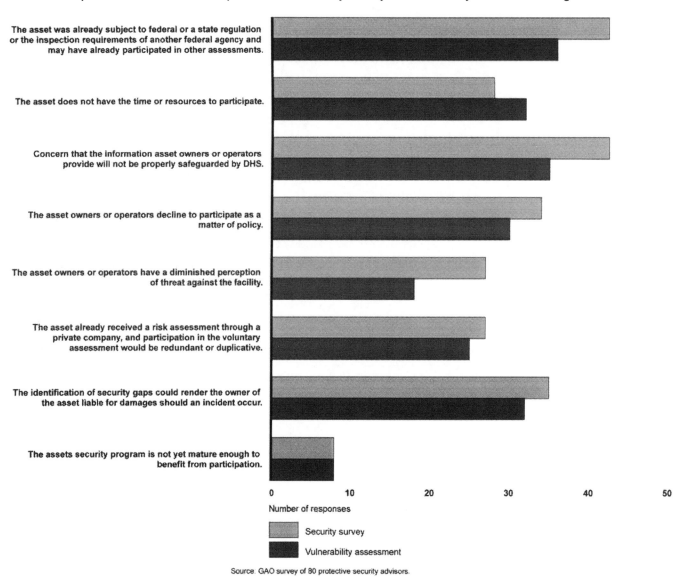

Figure 2: Frequencies with Which PSAs Reported Either "Often" or "Sometimes" Hearing Selected Reasons Why Asset Owners and Operators Declined to Participate in DHS's Security Survey or Vulnerability Assessment Programs

Number of responses

Security survey

Vulnerability assessment

Source: GAO survey of 80 protective security advisors.

While these PSA perceptions may reflect some reasons asset owners and operators decline to participate, it is important that DHS systematically identify reasons why high-priority asset owners and operators may decline to participate, especially if reasons differ from PSA

GAO-12-378 Critical Infrastructure Protection

region to PSA region or by sector or subsector. By doing so, DHS may be able to assess which declinations are within DHS's ability to control or influence and strategize how the security survey and vulnerability assessment program and DHS's approach toward promoting it can be modified to overcome any barriers identified. For example, 39 percent (31 of 80) of the PSAs who responded to our survey suggested that senior-level partners, including senior leaders within DHS, could better support the promotion of the security survey program when those leaders interact with CIKR partners at high-level meetings.[38] According to DHS, NPPD and IP officials meet often with nonfederal security partners, including sector coordinating councils (SCC), industry trade associations, state and local agencies, and private companies, to discuss the security survey and vulnerability assessment and other programs to assist in educating mission partners about the suite of available IP tools and resources. Meeting with security partners to discuss IP's surveys, assessments, and other programs is consistent with the NIPP partnership model whereby DHS officials in headquarters are to promote vulnerability assessments at high-level meetings where corporate owners are present—such as at SCC or Federal Senior Leadership Council meetings—and through the SSAs responsible for sector security. The NIPP also calls for DHS to rely on senior-level partners, such as the SCCs and state representatives, to create a coordinated national framework for CIKR protection and resilience within and across sectors and with industry representatives that includes the promotion of risk management activities, such as vulnerability assessments. Given the barriers to participation identified in our PSA survey, we contacted officials with 12 industry trade associations representing the water, commercial facilities, dams, and energy sectors to get their views on their awareness of DHS security surveys and vulnerability assessments. Officials representing 10 of the 12 trade associations said that they were aware of DHS's voluntary survey and vulnerability assessment programs, but only 6 of 12 knew if some of their members' had participated in these programs.

As noted earlier, at the time of our review DHS was not systematically collecting data on reasons why some owners and operators of high-priority assets decline to participate in security surveys or vulnerability assessments. Officials stated that they realize that some of the data

---

[38] Around 24 percent (19 of 80) of PSAs made similar comments regarding support for vulnerability assessments.

necessary to best manage these programs are not currently being collected and said that one example is that PSAs are not consistently reporting assessment and survey declinations from assets. DHS officials added that in an effort to increase efficiency and accuracy, they are developing additional data protocols to ensure that all the applicable data are being collected and considered to provide a more holistic understanding of the programs. Given that DHS efforts are just beginning, however, it is too early to assess the extent to which they will address these data collection challenges. Nevertheless, by developing a mechanism to systematically collect data on the reasons for declinations, consistent with DHS guidelines, DHS could be better positioned to identify common trends for such declinations, determine what programmatic and strategic actions are needed to manage participation among high-priority assets, and develop action plans with time frames and milestones to serve as a road map for addressing any problems. This could enhance the overall protection and resilience of those high-priority CIKR assets crucial to national security, public health and safety, and the economy. Given that DHS officials recognize the need to collect these data to obtain a more holistic understanding of these programs, DHS could be better positioned if it had a plan, with time frames and milestones, for developing and implementing these protocols. Standard practices for project management state that managing a project involves, among other things, developing a plan with time frames and milestones to identify points throughout the process to reassess efforts under way to determine whether project changes are necessary.[39] By having plan with time frames and milestones for developing additional data protocols, IP could be better positioned to provide a more complete picture of its effort to develop and complete this task. This could also provide DHS managers and other decision makers with (1) insights into IP's overall progress and (2) a basis for determining what, if any, additional actions need to be taken.

---

[39] Project Management Institute, *The Standard for Program Management©*.

DHS Shares Survey and Assessment Results with Asset Owners and Operators and Sector-Specific Agencies but Faces Challenges

DHS shares security survey and vulnerability assessment information with asset owners and operators that participate in these programs and shares aggregated sector information with SSAs. However, DHS faces challenges ensuring that this information is shared with asset owners and operators in a timely manner and in providing SSAs security survey-derived products that can help SSAs in their sector security roles. According to DHS officials, they are working to overcome these challenges, but it is unclear whether DHS actions will address SSA concerns about the use of aggregate security survey data.

Security Survey and Vulnerability Assessment Results Can Be Useful in Helping Asset Owners and Operators Reduce Risk

DHS security surveys and vulnerability assessments can provide valuable insights into the strengths and weaknesses of assets and can help asset owners and operators make decisions about investments to enhance security and resilience. For example, our survey of PSAs showed that most PSAs believe that the survey dashboard and the vulnerability assessment were moderately to very useful tools for reducing risk at CIKR assets. Specifically, 89 percent of PSAs (71 of 80) and 83 percent of PSAs (66 of 80) responded that the security surveys and vulnerability assessments, respectively, were moderately to very useful products for reducing risk. One PSA commented that "The dashboard is the first tool of its kind that allows the owner/operator a clear and measurable quantitative picture of existing security profile" while another commented that "[Vulnerability assessments] provide specific, actionable items for the owner/operator to take action on to decrease vulnerabilities."

Our discussions with various CIKR stakeholders—specifically asset owners and operators and SSA representatives—also showed that these tools can be useful to the asset owners and operators that participate in these programs. As will be discussed later in greater detail, 6 of the 10 asset owners and operators we contacted used the results of these survey and assessment tools to support proposals for security changes at the assets that had been assessed. As one owner and operator said, these voluntary programs provide a fresh look at facility security from a holistic perspective. Another asset operator told us that it is nice to be able to see how its security practices compare to those of others within its sector. The representatives of the four SSAs we spoke with also believe the security survey and vulnerability assessments were beneficial to the asset owners and operators that received them.

DHS Is Not Delivering Results to Owners and Operators in a Timely Manner

The usefulness of security survey and vulnerability assessment results could be enhanced by the timely delivery of these products to the owners and operators that participated in them. For example, facility owners may not see the importance of an identified security weakness if they do not receive this information soon after a security survey or vulnerability assessment is completed. Furthermore, the inability to deliver results within the expected time frame could undermine the relationship DHS is attempting to develop with asset owners and operators. As mentioned earlier, PSAs rely on Argonne National Laboratory to provide them with the results of the vulnerability assessments, which PSAs, in turn, deliver directly to asset owners and operators. While PSAs find the voluntary programs useful, 14 percent of PSAs we surveyed (11 of 80) described late delivery of the reports as a factor that undermines the usefulness of vulnerability assessments. One PSA commented that "the program is broken in regard to timely completion of reports and deliverables (protective measures and resiliency dashboards) for the asset owners/operators. I have yet to receive anything from (a vulnerability assessment conducted several months ago). I have not even received the draft report for review nor the dashboard. This creates a big credibility problem for me with my stakeholders who are looking for the results." The NIPP states that in order to have an effective environment for information sharing, CIKR partners need to be provided with timely and relevant information that they can use to make decisions. Consistent with the NIPP, DHS guidelines state that PSAs are to provide the results of security surveys in the form of a survey dashboard within 30 days of when the security survey was completed. In addition, according to PSCD officials, although there is no written guidance, PSCD expects that vulnerability assessment results are to be provided to assets within 60 days of completion of the vulnerability assessment.

We analyzed DHS LENS data to determine the extent to which survey dashboards were delivered to asset owners and operators on a timely basis, using DHS's 30-day criteria for timeliness. Our analysis showed that for fiscal year 2011, more than half of all dashboards and vulnerability assessment reports were delivered to owners and operators late.[40] Specifically, of the 570 dashboard reports that were supposed to

---

[40] The LENS database did not contain a data field to capture the delivery date of the dashboard to the facility until January 2011, but the database did contain a tracking field for vulnerability assessment delivery for fiscal years 2009 through 2011. Therefore, we limited our analysis of dashboard deliveries for security surveys to fiscal year 2011, which contains the most complete delivery data in LENS, and limited our analysis of vulnerability assessment reports to the same parameters.

be delivered during fiscal year 2011, about 24 percent (139 of 570) were delivered on time and approximately 60 percent (344 of 570) were late, with almost half of those delivered 30 days beyond the 30-day deadline established by DHS guidelines. Data were missing for about 15 percent (85 of 570) of the remaining dashboards.[41] Figure 3 shows the timeliness of dashboard deliveries for all security surveys conducted in fiscal year 2011.

Figure 3: Timeliness of Security Survey Dashboards Delivered to Asset Owners and Operators during Fiscal Year 2011

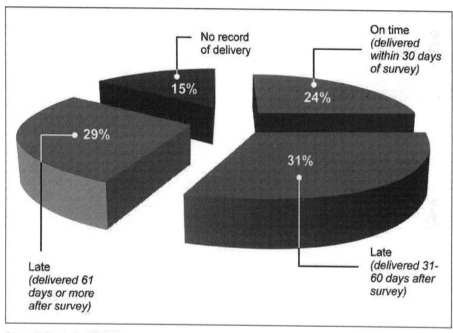

Source: GAO analysis of DHS data.
Note: "No record of delivery" means that these records within the LENS database did not contain any data in the delivery date field. Percentages do not add to 100 because of rounding.

With regard to vulnerability assessment reports, our analysis likewise showed that the majority of these products had been delivered to owners

---

[41] Percentages do not add to 100 because of rounding. We were not able to use data for 2 of the 570 dashboards in our analysis. As discussed earlier in this report, we could not ascertain which facilities among all of those that underwent a security survey were high-priority assets because of limitations associated with matching LENs data with the NCIPP list. Nonetheless, the extent to which LENS data showed that dashboards were late corroborates the views of PSAs who expressed concerns about lateness.

GAO-12-378 Critical Infrastructure Protection

and operators later than the guidelines established by DHS officials specified. Our analysis of LENS data for fiscal year 2011 showed that DHS had conducted 206 vulnerability assessments. Using the 60-day criteria articulated by DHS officials, we found that about 13 percent (26 of 206) of the vulnerability assessment reports were delivered to the asset representatives within 60 days and approximately 33 percent (67 of 206) were delivered up to 60 days late. An additional 51 percent (105 of 206) of vulnerability assessments were delivered more than 60 days late. We were unable to determine the date delivered for about 4 percent (8 of 206) of the deliveries because of missing data in the LENS database.[42] Figure 4 shows the extent to which LENS data show the timeliness of vulnerability assessment reports delivered to asset owners and operators during fiscal year 2011.

Figure 4: Timeliness of Vulnerability Assessment Reports Delivered to Asset Owners and Operators during Fiscal Year 2011

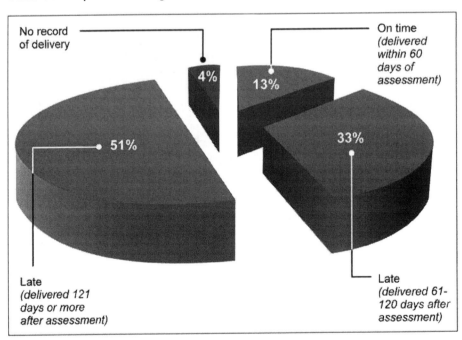

No record of delivery — 4%

On time (delivered within 60 days of assessment) — 13%

Late (delivered 61-120 days after assessment) — 33%

Late (delivered 121 days or more after assessment) — 51%

Source: GAO analysis of DHS data.
Note: "No record of delivery" means that these records within the LENS database did not contain any data in the delivery date field. Percentages do not add to 100 because of rounding.

---

[42] Percentages do not add to 100 because of rounding.

GAO-12-378 Critical Infrastructure Protection

DHS officials told us that there were several possible reasons why asset owners and operators did not receive dashboards or vulnerability assessment reports within the time frames established by DHS. First, they said they were clearing a backlog of vulnerability assessment reports that resulted from, among other things, changes to the program's quality assurance process and that because of the backlog, delivery of these reports could take as long as 6 months. Second, DHS officials explained that a direct delivery to the asset representative requires that both the owner or operator's representative and the PSA be available to meet because the PSA not only delivers the product but meets with the representative at that time to explain how the product can benefit the asset. Third, DHS officials said that it is possible that PSAs are entering delivery information into LENS late or not at all. DHS officials could not estimate how often this was occurring. However, they said LENS has built-in reminders to encourage the PSA to record delivery of the security survey and vulnerability assessment products in a timely manner. They also said that after a product is available for delivery to asset representatives, the PSA is sent automated reminders to record the delivery date in LENS and the PSA receives these reminders until the date of delivery is recorded.

Representatives of 9 of the 10 high-priority assets whom we contacted participated in either the security survey or assessment, and 8 of the 9 had received either a dashboard or a vulnerability assessment report. These representatives had mixed reviews of the DHS security survey and vulnerability assessment programs, including the timeliness of dashboards and vulnerability assessment reports. Officials representing 6 of the 8 assets who had received a dashboard or vulnerability assessment report said they used the results of surveys or assessments to support proposals to make security improvements. Officials representing one asset told us that they found the dashboard extremely valuable because it showed how the security of their asset compared to that of like assets. Representatives of 2 of the participating assets had not yet received the results for the survey or assessment. At 1 of these assets, the officials representing the asset had not received a vulnerability assessment report 7 months after completion of the assessment. We later learned that this asset received its report shortly after our visit, and the representative told us that it was both informative and educational. At the other asset, officials told us that a dashboard had not been provided 10 months after the asset participated in a security survey. Furthermore, this representative did not remember hearing of the dashboard and did not realize that the asset was supposed to receive a product as a result of completing the security survey.

GAO-12-378 Critical Infrastructure Protection

Standards for Internal Control in the Federal Government states that pertinent information should be identified, captured, and distributed in a form and time frame that permits people to perform their duties efficiently. The late delivery of security survey dashboards and vulnerability assessment reports delays the participating assets from making use of this information in their security planning. By taking actions to ensure that security survey results and vulnerability assessment reports are delivered in a timely fashion, consistent with DHS guidelines and the NIPP, asset owners and operators could have better information with which to make decisions about security enhancements and DHS might be able to realize ancillary benefits associated with enhancing perceptions about its security survey and vulnerability assessment programs. IP officials acknowledged that the delivery of survey dashboards and vulnerability reports to assets has not been as timely as it should be. They said that in an effort to increase timeliness, IP is working with contractors and program staff to improve the processes and protocols that govern the delivery of assessment and survey products to assets. However, IP officials did not elaborate on the specific actions they were taking with their contractors and program staff or their road map for doing so, consistent with project management practices previously discussed.[43] By developing a plan with time frames and specific milestones for completing improvements that govern the delivery of surveys and assessments, IP could be better positioned to provide a more complete picture of its approach for developing and completing these tasks. These plans could also provide DHS managers and other decision makers insights into IP's overall progress in completing these tasks and provide a basis for determining what, if any, additional actions need to be taken.

Unclear Whether DHS Actions to Enhance Sharing of Survey and Assessment Results Will Address Concerns Raised by Sector-Specific Agencies

In addition to sharing the results of security surveys and vulnerability assessments with individual asset owners and operators (as discussed in the previous section), DHS also shares results with SSAs. Specifically, DHS shares information with SSAs that includes aggregate security survey results for each sector and is taking action to enhance the information it provides, but it is unclear whether these actions will resolve SSA concerns about the completeness and validity of the aggregated results. According to the NIPP, DHS is responsible for establishing and maintaining a comprehensive, multitiered, dynamic information-sharing

---

[43] Project Management Institute, *The Standard for Program Management©*.

network designed to provide assessments, among other information, to public and private sector partners. Furthermore, the NIPP states that SSAs are responsible for working with DHS and other government agency representatives to develop protective programs, resilience strategies, and related requirements and that SSAs are to report priorities for CIKR protection in the sector annual reports and sector-specific plans.

Beginning in 2009, DHS used results of security surveys to produce summaries for SSAs.[44] According to DHS, the purpose of these summaries was to provide SSA officials with an overall picture of sector security and vulnerability and help them develop plans and reports for their sectors. These summaries contained DHS contact information, but according to DHS officials, none of the SSAs contacted them with questions or comments. According to the Deputy Director for PSCD, DHS did not make any additional effort to contact SSAs after these summary reports were distributed because he believed that DHS had shared information with stakeholders consistent with the NIPP. We subsequently contacted SSA officials representing four sectors—the commercial facilities, dams, energy, and water sectors—about their use of the sector summaries provided by DHS. They told us that they did not find the security survey sector summaries useful for understanding sector security and resiliency issues. They said that the usefulness of the DHS security survey was limited to the asset receiving the security survey rather than the sectors in aggregate. Officials at three out of the four SSAs told us they were concerned with the methodology used by DHS to calculate each sector's protective measures index, such as grouping all assets together, regardless of size or importance and averaging the security survey scores. An official at the fourth SSA said that he was not comfortable with the data and did not believe that enough security surveys were performed in the sector to provide an understanding of sector security strengths and weaknesses. We shared this information with DHS officials, and they emphasized that the security surveys and vulnerability assessments are primarily intended for use by assets and state and local partners. However, they noted that officials from the commercial facilities and dams SSAs—two sectors for which DHS is the

---

[44] In 2009, DHS produced sector summaries for the following sectors: banking and finance, commercial facilities, dams, defense industrial base, emergency services, energy, government facilities, health care and public health, postal and shipping, transportation, and water. In 2010, DHS provided security survey summaries for each of the 18 sectors.

GAO-12-378 Critical Infrastructure Protection

SSA—have requested access to the summary data generated from these activities.

DHS is aware of concerns regarding aggregate survey results and has begun to take action to revise its approach to sharing them with SSAs. For example, DHS did not include security survey summary data in the 2010 NAR after SSA officials raised concerns that the security survey data were not sufficient to accurately assess the security posture of a sector and that data should not be compared between sectors because of sector differences.[45] DHS also issued revised security survey sector summaries in 2011 that included protective measures statistics for subsectors and an "options for consideration" section with specific protective measures adopted by the top 20 percent of assets in subsectors (as measured by the overall score for these assets).[46] According to the sector summaries, this information was intended for asset owners and operators to use to increase their security. However, officials also told us that these 2011 sector summaries were not distributed to SSAs but were available upon request. They added that they plan to discontinue the security survey sector summaries for 2012 and they will be replaced by a web-based dashboard tool, accessible to SSA officials and local sector partners. DHS officials told us that the web-based tool is currently under development and is to be released in January 2013. DHS officials provided a schedule that showed the various steps it plans to take from March 2012 through January 2013 to implement the tool. The schedule identified specific dates for further testing and improvement of the tool, but it did not identify any efforts to engage SSAs in this process.

In addition to its specific efforts to provide aggregate survey results and develop a web-based tool, DHS also surveyed SSA officials in 2010 to, among other things, understand and gauge the relevance, satisfaction, and effectiveness of IP's risk mitigation programs and to obtain a better understanding of the infrastructure protection needs and desires of IP

---

[45] According to the NIPP, DHS recommends priorities and requirements for CIKR protection to the Executive Office of the President through the NAR.

[46] DHS produced security survey sector summaries for 10 sectors in 2011: banking, commercial facilities, dams, emergency services, energy, food and agriculture, government facilities, health care, transportation, and water.

stakeholders.[47] The survey showed that SSA officials were uncertain about the effect these programs had on asset and sector security.[48] For example, 53 percent (42 of 79) of SSA officials responded "don't know" to a question regarding the effectiveness of DHS's security survey program. In addition, 29 percent (23 of 79) of the respondents rated the security survey program as good or excellent at reducing risk. In response, DHS officials said that they have used these survey results to make program changes, such as integrating more SSAs into its RRAP activities starting in FY 2011. They also noted that 2 of the 18 SSAs had participated in a January 2012 meeting to identify stakeholder needs for security survey data where the web-based tool was discussed and feedback was provided. However, based on the information provided on the development of web-based tool, it is unclear how it will improve the understanding of sector-level security and resiliency. As of May 2012, DHS did not yet have details of what the future web-based tool would offer to SSAs.

DHS actions to survey SSAs to obtain their views about various aspects of IP's risk mitigation programs and engage 2 of the 18 SSAs on their needs regarding the web-based tool are consistent with the NIPP, which states that when the government is provided with an understanding of information needs, it can adjust its information collection, analysis, synthesis, and sharing accordingly. In October 2005, we reported that to achieve a common outcome, collaborating agencies need to establish strategies that work in concert with those of their partners or are joint in nature.[49] Such strategies help align the partner agencies' activities, core processes, and resources to accomplish the common outcome. Through its outreach and engagement with CIKR partners, DHS could work with its partners to help them enhance sector security and resiliency. Given that SSAs are key players in the overall NIPP partnership framework, DHS could be better positioned to develop a more robust web-based tool by

---

[47] SSA officials from all 18 sectors were interviewed using a questionnaire containing a mix of 139 closed- and open-ended questions. These results were in included in a briefing titled *IP Stakeholder Input Project: SSA Interview Findings Briefing*, January 5, 2011.

[48] IP officials administered the survey of SSA officials. IP solicited information from all IP divisions to understand what issues to address in the questionnaire. However, security survey summaries were not mentioned in the survey questionnaire.

[49] GAO, *Results-Oriented Government: Practices That Can Help Enhance and Sustain Collaboration among Federal Agencies*, GAO-06-15 (Washington, D.C.: Oct. 21, 2005).

revising its plans to reflect when and how it intends to engage SSAs in designing, testing, and implementing the tool, consistent with the NIPP and standards for project management.[50] By doing so, DHS could be better positioned to help ensure that it addresses any lingering concerns SSAs have about the use of aggregated security survey and vulnerability assessment data before the tool is finalized.

DHS Could Better Measure Security Survey and Vulnerability Assessment Results to Improve Program Management

DHS has taken actions to determine whether asset owners or operators have made security improvements based on the results of security surveys. However, DHS has not developed an overall approach to determine (1) the extent to which changes have enhanced asset protection and resilience over time or (2) why asset owners and operators do not make enhancements that would help mitigate vulnerabilities identified during security surveys and vulnerability assessments. As a result, DHS may be overlooking an opportunity to make improvements in the management of its voluntary risk mitigation programs that could also help DHS work with asset owners and operators to improve security and resilience. According to DHS, moving forward, it may consider changes to the types of information gathered as part of its effort to measure improvements, but it has not considered what additional information, if any, should be gathered from asset owners or operators that participate in security surveys and vulnerability assessments.

DHS Has Implemented a Security Survey Follow-up Tool

According to the NIPP, the use of performance measures is a critical step in the risk management process to enable DHS to objectively and quantitatively assess improvement in CIKR protection and resiliency at the sector and national levels. The NIPP states that the use of performance metrics provides a basis for DHS to establish accountability, document actual performance, promote effective management, and provide a feedback mechanism to decision makers. Consistent with the NIPP, DHS has taken action to follow up with security survey participants to gather feedback from asset owners and operators that participated in the program regarding the effect these programs have had on asset security using a standardized data collection tool, hereafter referred to as the follow-up tool or tool.

---

[50] Project Management Institute, *The Standard for Program Management*©.

DHS first began to do follow-ups with asset owners and operators in May 2010 but suspended its follow-up activities shortly thereafter to make enhancements to the tool it used.[51] In January 2011, IP introduced its revised follow-up tool, which was to be used by PSAs to ask asset representatives whose assets had undergone a security survey and received a dashboard about enhancements made in six general categories—information sharing, security management, security force, protective measures, physical security, and dependencies. Whereas the original follow-up tool focused on changes asset owners and operators made to enhance security and resilience, the revised tool focused on changes that were made directly as a result of DHS security surveys. According to DHS guidance, the tool was to be used 180 days after the completion of a security survey at an asset. The tool, which directs PSAs to ask a series of questions about improvements made as a result of the survey, instructs PSAs to request information on specific enhancements within those categories that were discussed in the dashboard provided to the asset owners and operators. For example, within the physical security category, the tool instructs the PSAs to ask about any enhancements to things like fences, gates, parking, lighting, and access control, among others, and to ask asset owners or operators whether an identified change was made as a result of the security survey the asset had received. In February 2011, shortly after the revised tool was introduced, IP issued guidelines that instructed PSAs to implement the follow-up tool. According to IP officials, PSAs used the tool to follow up with owners and operators of 610 assets from January 2011 through September 2011. Data provided by IP showed that about 21 percent (126 of the 610) of the respondents to the PSA follow-ups reported that they had completed improvements, and 81 percent of these (102 of 126) reported that those improvements were implemented as the result of the security survey the asset received. According to IP's data, the most common types of improvements identified by assets that had completed improvements since receiving the security survey were changes to information sharing, which could include activities such as participating in working groups, and physical security.

---

[51] See GAO-10-772. In September 2010, we reported that DHS had initiated a process to follow up with asset owners and operators to track the extent to which they had made improvements following their participation in the survey.

GAO-12-378 Critical Infrastructure Protection

Follow-up Data on Results Do Not Reflect Long-Term Program Performance

DHS guidance states that PSAs are to conduct a follow-up with the asset owners and operators 180 days after an asset receives a security survey. We compared DHS data on 522 security surveys conducted from July 1, 2010, through March 31, 2011, with DHS data on the follow-ups performed from January 1, 2011, through September 30, 2011—180 days after DHS completed the security surveys. We found that DHS did not contact some asset owners or operators that should have received a 180-day follow-up and contacted some owners and operators that had participated in a security survey more than 180 days prior to the introduction of the tool. For example, of the 522 security survey participants that participated in a security survey from July 1, 2010, through March 31, 2011, 208 (40 percent) received the 180-day follow-up and 314 (60 percent) did not. Furthermore, DHS recorded an additional 402 follow-ups on assets that had received their security survey more than 180 days prior to the introduction of the tool. Thus, the data DHS reported included improvements assets made beyond the 180-day scope of the follow-up tool, making it difficult to measure the effectiveness of the security survey in prompting enhancements within 180 days of the survey.

According to PSCD officials, there are two key reasons why DHS used the follow-up tool to capture data on changes made beyond 180 days. First, program officials said that completion of the 180-day follow-up depends upon the asset representative's willingness to participate and availability to answer these questions. If the asset representative does not agree to participate, or neither the representative nor the PSA is available, the 180-day follow-up cannot be completed on schedule. However, when DHS provided the follow-up data in November 2011, officials said that they were not aware of any asset owners or operators that had refused to participate in the 180-day follow-up at that time. Second, program officials noted that the inclusion of assets that had received a security survey more than 180 days prior to the introduction of the revised follow-up tool occurred because they believed that it was necessary to capture data on as many assets as possible. They said that IP intends that follow-ups be completed as close to the 180-day mark as possible, but they believed it was important to initially document whether the security survey resulted in changes to security, regardless of when the change was made. IP officials further explained that they had developed a similar follow-up tool to capture data on enhancements resulting from vulnerability assessments. However, at the time of our review, results were not available from the vulnerability assessment follow-up tool, which was also implemented in January 2011 and was designed to capture data on enhancements made 365 days following the delivery of the vulnerability assessment report. Consistent with the security survey, DHS officials explained that the 365-day follow-up for vulnerability assessments was determined as a means to begin the process of collecting and assessing data on improvements being made as a result of the assessments. They added that as more data are collected, IP will review the information to determine if the follow-up visits for security surveys and vulnerability assessments should remain at 180 and 365 days, respectively, or be moved as a result of information collected from asset owners and operators. Nonetheless, DHS officials did not provide a road map with time frames and milestones showing when they planned to revisit the 180-day follow-up time frame or the intervals between follow-ups. Consistent with the standards for project management, by having a road map with time frames and milestones for revisiting these time frames, IP could be better positioned to provide a more complete picture of its overall progress making these decisions and a basis for determining what, if any, additional actions need to be taken or data inputs need to be made.[52]

Expanding the scope and time frame of the follow-up tool is consistent with the NIPP risk management approach whereby performance measures are to enable DHS and the SSAs to objectively and quantitatively assess improvement in CIKR protection and resiliency. Furthermore, asset representatives we spoke with agree with the idea of conducting follow-up surveys over a longer time frame. Specifically, we asked representatives of the 10 assets we visited whether 180 days was enough time for changes to be made to assets, consistent with improvements identified by each asset based on DHS's security survey. Six of the 10 asset representatives responded that such a time frame would capture only the most basic of security improvements and that the planning and implementation of security improvements takes much longer than 180 days. The other 4 representatives did not comment. *Standards for Internal Control in the Federal Government* states that pertinent information should be identified and captured in a form and time frame that permits people to perform their duties efficiently.[53] By gathering data on security improvements over longer periods of time, or at intervals beyond the initial follow-up time frame, DHS could be positioned to better measure the effectiveness of its security survey program. This is

---

[52] Project Management Institute, *The Standard for Program Management©*.

[53] GAO/AIMD-00-21.3.1.

especially true if asset owners and operators are implementing more complicated enhancements over a longer term because of the need to develop and fund plans for particular types of improvements. For example, gathering these data could help DHS measure not only what improvements asset operators are implementing, but also how long it takes to complete the planning phase of a security enhancement project and how this time frame might vary by the type of improvement.

Furthermore, while it is important to capture information about improvements made as a result of these activities over time, it is also important that DHS either capture the information within the prescribed times outlined in DHS guidance, adjust the time frames based on an analysis of data captured over time, or perform follow-ups at additional intervals beyond those initially performed. This would also be consistent with *Standards for Internal Control in the Federal Government*, which calls for the establishment and review of performance measures and indicators to monitor activities and top-level reviews by management to track major agency achievements and compare these with plans, goals, and objectives.[54] By doing so, IP could be better positioned to document actual performance, promote effective management, provide a feedback mechanism to decision makers, and enhance overall accountability.

Additional Enhancements Could Better Position DHS to Measure Performance

According to DHS officials, moving forward, DHS may consider additional changes to its follow-up tool depending on the results they gather over time. The NIPP states that performance measures that focus on outputs, called output measures, such as whether an asset completes a security improvement, should track the progression of a task. The NIPP further states that outcome measures are to track progress toward an intended goal by beneficial results rather than level of activity. Our review of DHS's approach for following up with assets that had undergone a security survey showed that PSAs were instructed to focus on security enhancements completed as result of the security survey, not enhancements that were planned or in process. Nonetheless, our review of DHS's follow-up results for the period from January through September 2011 showed that DHS reported the following:

---

[54] GAO/AIMD-00-21.3.1.

- 41 percent (250 of 610) of the owners and operators surveyed reported that security enhancements were either in process or planned and
- the results did not indicate whether these planned or in-process enhancements were attributable to DHS's security survey at these assets.

After we discussed our observation with DHS officials, they informed us that they believe completed improvements are the best initial measurement of the impact of security surveys and vulnerability assessments. They added that other metrics can be added as the process matures and is refined. However, as of March 2012, DHS did not document whether planned or in-process improvements are the result of security surveys. Given that the NIPP calls for CIKR partners to measure performance in the context of the progression of the task, DHS could be missing an opportunity to measure performance associated with planned and in-process enhancements, especially if they are attributable to DHS efforts via security surveys and vulnerability assessments. DHS could also use this opportunity to consider how it can capture key information that could be used to understand why certain improvements were or were not made by assets owners and operators that have received surveys and assessments. For example, the follow-up tool could ask asset representatives

- what factors—such as cost, vulnerability, or perception of threat—influenced the decision to implement changes, either immediately or over time if they chose to make improvements;
- what factors—such as perception of risk, cost, or budget constraints—influenced an asset owner or operator to choose to not make any improvements;
- why were the improvements made chosen over other possible improvements, if improvements were made; and
- did the improvements, if any, involve the adoption of new or more cost-effective techniques that might be useful as an option for other owners and operators to consider as they explore the feasibility making improvements?

Understanding why an asset owner or operator chooses to make, or not make, improvements to its security is valuable information for understanding the obstacles asset owners or operators face when making security investments. For example, the cost of security upgrades can be a barrier to making enhancements. As one PSA who responded to our survey commented, "there is no requirement for the owner/operator to take action. They are left with making a "risk-reward" decision. Some see great value in making security upgrades, while others are less inclined to make improvements due to costs." Likewise, one asset representative told us that security is one of the most important things to management until budget time. In this regard, a better understanding of the complexity of the security improvement decision at the asset could also help DHS better understand the constraints asset owners or operators face in making these decisions—information that could possibly help DHS determine how, if at all, to refine its security survey program to assist asset owners or operators in making these decisions. For example, the NIPP states that effective CIKR programs and strategies seek to use resources efficiently by focusing on actions that offer the greatest mitigation of risk for any given expenditure. Additional information on the cost of improvements made and the reasons why improvements were or were not made could also assist DHS in understanding the trade-offs asset owners and operators face when making decisions to address vulnerabilities identified as a result of DHS security surveys and enhancements. IP officials told us they are wary of attempting to gather too much information from asset representatives with the follow-up tool because of a concern that being too intrusive may damage the relationships that the PSAs have established with asset representatives. They said that gathering additional information is not as important as maintaining strong relationships with the asset representatives.

We recognize that DHS operates its security survey program in a voluntary environment and that DHS can only succeed at improving asset and sector security if asset owners and operators are willing to participate, consistent with DHS's interest in maintaining good relationships with asset representatives. However, by gathering more information from assets that participate in these programs—particularly high-priority assets—DHS could be better positioned to measure the impact of its programs on critical infrastructure security at the sector and national levels. Moreover, by collecting and analyzing this type of information, DHS could be better informed in making decisions about whether adjustments to its voluntary programs are needed to make them more beneficial to CIKR assets—a factor which could help DHS further promote participation by asset owners and operators that may previously have been reluctant to participate in DHS security surveys and assessments. Having this type of information could also be important in light of DHS's efforts to better understand interdependencies between assets via the RRAPs. For instance, by knowing what factors influence decisions to make an improvement, or not, at one asset or a group of assets, DHS could be better positioned to understand how that decision influences the security of other assets that are also part of the RRAP. As a result, DHS and PSAs could then be better positioned to work with owners and operators to mitigate any vulnerabilities arising out of these decisions. It could also help DHS develop and target strategies for addressing why certain enhancements were not made and ultimately put DHS in a better position to measure outcomes, rather than outputs, associated with its efforts to promote protection and resilience via its voluntary risk mitigation programs.

Conclusions

DHS has taken important actions to conduct voluntary CIKR security surveys and vulnerability assessments, provide information to CIKR stakeholders, and assess the effectiveness of security surveys and vulnerability assessments. However, further actions could enhance each of these endeavors and provide DHS managers the information they need to ensure that IP is taking appropriate steps toward completing them or making adjustments where needed. DHS has not institutionalized realistic goals that could help DHS measure the effects of its efforts to promote and conduct security surveys and vulnerability assessments among high-priority assets. By developing realistic institutional goals, DHS could, for example, better measure the effects of its efforts to promote and conduct security surveys and vulnerability assessments among high-priority assets. Further, developing a road map with milestones and time frames for (1) taking and completing actions needed to resolve issues associated with data inconsistencies and matching data on the list of high-priority assets with data used to track the conduct of security surveys and vulnerability assessments, (2) completing protocols to systematically collect data on the reasons why some owners and operators declined to participate in the voluntary surveys and assessments, and (3) improving the timely delivery of the results of security surveys and vulnerability assessments could better position DHS to target high-priority assets and provide them with the information they need to make decisions related to security and resiliency. Moreover, by revising its plans to include when and how SSAs will be engaged in designing, testing, and implementing the web-based tool, consistent with its recent efforts to coordinate with CIKR partners, DHS could be positioned to better understand and address their information needs.

Consistent with the NIPP, DHS is also continuing to take actions to follow up with asset owners and operators that have participated in security surveys and vulnerability assessments to gauge the extent to which these surveys and assessments have prompted owners and operators to improve security and resilience at their assets. DHS officials said that they intend to review the information it gathers from asset owners and operators to determine if the follow-up visits should remain at 180 days after DHS completed the security surveys. By establishing a road map with milestones and time frames for conducting this review, DHS would be better positioned to provide a picture of its overall progress in making these decisions and a basis for determining what, if any, additional actions need to be taken or data inputs need to be made and whether additional follow-ups are appropriate at intervals beyond the follow-ups initially performed. In addition, collecting detailed data on actions started and planned and, for example, why actions were not taken, could provide DHS valuable information on the decision-making process associated with making security enhancements and enable DHS to better understand what barriers owners and operators face in making improvements to the security of their assets.

Recommendations for Executive Action

To better ensure that DHS's efforts to promote security surveys and vulnerability assessments among high-priority CIKR are aligned with institutional goals, that the information gathered through these surveys and assessments meet the needs of stakeholders, and that DHS is positioned to know how these surveys and assessments could be improved, we recommend that the Assistant Secretary for Infrastructure Protection, Department of Homeland Security, take the following seven actions:

- develop plans with milestones and time frames to resolve issues associated with data inconsistencies and matching data on the list of high-priority assets with data used to track the conduct of security surveys and vulnerability assessments;
- institutionalize realistic performance goals for appropriate levels of participation in security surveys and vulnerability assessments by high-priority assets to measure how well DHS is achieving its goals;
- design and implement a mechanism for systematically assessing why owners and operators of high-priority assets decline to participate and a develop a road map, with time frames and milestones, for completing this effort;
- develop time frames and specific milestones for managing DHS's efforts to ensure the timely delivery of the results of security surveys and vulnerability assessments to asset owners and operators;
- revise its plans to include when and how SSAs will be engaged in designing, testing, and implementing DHS's web-based tool to address and mitigate any SSA concerns that may arise before the tool is finalized;

- develop a road map with time frames and specific milestones for reviewing the information it gathers from asset owners and operators to determine if follow-up visits should remain at 180 days for security surveys and whether additional follow-ups are appropriate at intervals beyond the follow-ups initially performed; and
- consider the feasibility of expanding the follow-up program to gather and act upon data, as appropriate, on (1) security enhancements that are ongoing and planned that are attributable to DHS security surveys and vulnerability assessments and (2) factors, such as cost and perceptions of threat, that influence asset owner and operator decisions to make, or not make, enhancements based on the results of DHS security surveys and vulnerability assessments.

Agency Comments and Our Evaluation

We provided a draft of this report to the Secretary of Homeland Security for review and comment. In its written comments reprinted in appendix IV, DHS agreed with all seven of the recommendations; however, its implementation plans do not fully address two of these seven recommendations and it is unclear to what extent its plans will address two other recommendations.

With regard to the first recommendation that DHS develop plans to resolve issues associated with data inconsistencies between its databases, DHS stated its efforts to assign unique identifiers to assets on the high-priority list that have received security surveys and vulnerability assessments will make matching easier and that other quality assurance processes have been implemented to better verify individual asset data. We agree these are positive steps; however, to fully address the recommendation, we believe DHS should develop a plan with time frames and milestones that specify how the steps it says it is taking address the data inconsistencies we cited, and demonstrate the results—how many high-priority assets received security surveys, vulnerability assessments, or both in a given year—of that effort. By doing so, DHS would be better positioned to provide a more complete picture of its approach for developing and completing these tasks. It would also provide DHS managers and other decision makers with insights into (1) IP's overall progress in completing these tasks and (2) a basis for determining what, if any, additional actions need to be taken.

With regard to the second recommendation that DHS institutionalize realistic performance goals for levels of participation in security surveys and vulnerability assessments by high-priority assets, DHS stated that the participation of high-priority assets continues to be a concern but reiterated its view that the voluntary nature of its programs and competing priorities makes setting goals for high-priority participation difficult. DHS stated that its fiscal year 2012 Project Management Plans for Protective Security Advisor and Vulnerability Assessment Projects established realistic goals concerning the total number of assessments to be conducted. However, they said these plans do not include goals for assessments performed at high-priority assets. Furthermore, DHS stated the shift in emphasis to regional resilience suggested metrics and goals intended to measure the participation of high-priority assets in vulnerability assessments and surveys may not be a strong or accurate indicator of the degree to which DHS is achieving its infrastructure protection and resilience goals. We agree that the voluntary nature of these programs and changing priorities make the process of setting goals difficult. However, the NIPP and DHS guidance emphasize the importance of high-priority participation in these programs, and DHS can take factors like the voluntary nature of the program and DHS's shift toward regional resilience into account when setting realistic goals for the number of security surveys and vulnerability assessments it conducts at high-priority facilities. By establishing realistic performance goals for levels of participation by high priority assets, DHS would be better positioned to compare actual performance against expected results and develop strategies for overcoming differences or adjust its goals to more realistically reflect the challenges it faces.

With regard to the third recommendation that DHS design and implement a mechanism for systematically assessing why owners and operators of high priority assets decline to participate and develop a road map, with time frames and milestones, for completing this effort, DHS stated it recognizes that additional clarification and guidance are needed to ensure effective implementation of existing guidance. Specifically, DHS stated it will review and revise the guidance to (1) determine if revisions to the existing process are required and (2) develop supplementary guidance to aid PSAs in executing the process. DHS stated it will initiate this review in the fourth quarter of fiscal year 2012, after which time it will develop additional milestones for mechanism improvement. We believe that DHS's proposed actions appear to be a step in the right direction, but it is too early to tell whether DHS's actions will result in an improved mechanism for systematically assessing why owners and operators decline to participate.

Regarding the fourth recommendation to develop time frames and specific milestones for managing its efforts to improve the timely delivery of the results of security surveys and vulnerability assessments to asset owners and operators, DHS stated it is working with contractors and program staff to advance the processes and protocols governing the delivery of assessment and survey products to facilities. DHS also stated that it had begun a review of assessments lacking delivery dates in LENS and is working with PSAs to populate the missing information. In addition, DHS noted that its plan to transition to a web-based dashboard system will help mitigate the issue of timely report delivery by eliminating the need for in-person delivery of the dashboard product. However, DHS did not discuss time frames and milestones for completing these efforts. Thus, it is unclear to what extent DHS's actions will fully address this recommendation. As noted in our report, developing time frames and milestones for completing improvements that govern the delivery of the results of surveys and assessments would provide insights into IP's overall progress.

With regard to the fifth recommendation to revise its plans to include when and how SSAs will be engaged in designing, testing, and implementing DHS's web-based tool, DHS stated that it is currently taking actions to develop and test a web-based dashboard tool for individual owners and operators, which is expected to be widely available in January 2013. DHS stated that it anticipates the development of a state and local "view," or dashboard, following the successful deployment of the web-based owner and operator dashboards. Regarding SSAs, DHS stated that a concept for a sector-level view of assessment data has been proposed and that the requirements and feasibility of such a dashboard will be explored more fully following the completion of the state-level web-based dashboard. DHS noted that that IP will engage the SSAs to determine any associated requirements. DHS's proposed actions appear to be a step in the right direction. However, given that the sector level view of assessment data is in the proposal stage and further action will be explored more fully after completion of the state level web-based dashboard, it is too early to tell when and how SSA's will be engaged in designing, testing and implementing the web-based tool.

In response to the sixth recommendation to develop a road map with time frames and specific milestones to determine if follow-up visits should remain at 180 days for security surveys, and whether additional follow-ups are appropriate at intervals beyond the follow-ups initially performed, DHS stated it will analyze and compare security survey follow-up results in early calendar year 2013 to determine whether modifications are required. DHS also stated that given that the 365-day follow-up process went into effect in January 2011, the first follow-up evaluations of vulnerability assessments have only recently begun and IP will collect, at a minimum, 1 year of vulnerability assessment data. DHS said that IP intends to review the results for both the security survey 180-day follow-up and the 365-day follow-up in early calendar year 2013 to determine whether modifications to the follow-up intervals are required. DHS's proposed actions are consistent with the intent of this recommendation.

In response to the seventh recommendation to consider the feasibility of gathering and acting upon additional data, where appropriate, on (1) ongoing or planned enhancements attributable to security surveys and assessments and (2) factors that influence asset owner and operator decisions to make or not make security enhancements, DHS stated that it collects information on ongoing or planned enhancements. However, as noted in the report, DHS does not collect information that would show whether these enhancements are attributable to security surveys and assessments. DHS also stated that IP will continue to work with Argonne National Laboratory and field personnel to determine the best method for collecting information related to those factors influencing an asset's decision to implement or not implement a new protective measure or security enhancement. However, it is not clear to what extent DHS's actions will fully address this recommendation because it did not discuss whether it will consider the feasibility of gathering data on whether ongoing or planned enhancements are attributable to security surveys and assessments or how it will act upon the data it currently gathers or plans to gather to, among other things, measure performance in the context of the progression of the task, consistent with the NIPP. By gathering and analyzing data on why an asset owner or operator chooses to make, or not make, improvement to security, DHS would be better positioned to understand the obstacles asset owners face when making investments.

DHS also provided technical comments, which we incorporated as appropriate.

As agreed with your offices, unless you publicly announce the contents of this report earlier, we plan no further distribution until 30 days from the report date. At that time, we will send copies to the Secretary of Homeland Security, the Under Secretary for the National Protection Programs Directorate, and other interested parties. In addition, the report will be available at no charge on the GAO website at http://www.gao.gov.

If you or your staff have questions about this report, please contact me at (202) 512-8777 or caldwells@gao.gov. Contact points for our Offices of

Congressional Relations and Public Affairs may be found on the last page of this report. Key contributors to this report are listed in appendix V.

Stephen L. Caldwell
Director, Homeland Security and Justice Issues

Appendix I: Critical Infrastructure Sectors

This appendix provides information on the 18 critical infrastructure sectors and the federal agencies responsible for sector security. The National Infrastructure Protection Plan (NIPP) outlines the roles and responsibilities of the Department of Homeland Security (DHS) and its partners—including other federal agencies. Within the NIPP framework, DHS is responsible for leading and coordinating the overall national effort to enhance protection via 18 critical infrastructure and key resources (CIKR) sectors. Homeland Security Presidential Directive (HSPD) 7 and the NIPP assign responsibility for CIKR sectors to sector-specific agencies (SSA). As an SSA, DHS has direct responsibility for leading, integrating, and coordinating efforts of sector partners to protect 11 of the 18 CIKR sectors. The remaining sectors are coordinated by eight other federal agencies. Table 2 lists the SSAs and their sectors.

Table 2: SSAs and CIKR Sectors

SSA	CIKR sector
Department of Agriculture[a] and Food and Drug Administration[b]	Food and agriculture
Department of Defense[c]	Defense industrial base
Department of Energy	Energy[d]
Department of Health and Human Services	Health care and public health
Department of the Interior	National monuments and icons
Department of the Treasury	Banking and finance
Environmental Protection Agency	Water[e]
Department of Homeland Security	
Office of Infrastructure Protection	Commercial facilities Critical manufacturing Emergency services Nuclear reactors, materials, and waste Dams Chemical
Office of Cyber Security and Communications	Information technology Communications
Transportation Security Administration	Postal and shipping
Transportation Security Administration and U. S. Coast Guard[f]	Transportation systems[g]
Federal Protective Service[h]	Government facilities[i]

Source: 2009 National Infrastructure Protection Plan.

[a]The Department of Agriculture is responsible for agriculture and food (meat, poultry, and egg products).

[b]The Food and Drug Administration is the part of the Department of Health and Human Services and is responsible for food other than meat, poultry, and egg products.

[c]Nothing in the NIPP impairs or otherwise affects the authority of the Secretary of Defense over the Department of Defense, including the chain of command for military forces from the President as Commander in Chief, to the Secretary of Defense, to the commanders of military forces, or military command and control procedures.

[d]The energy sector includes the production, refining, storage, and distribution of oil, gas, and electric power, except for commercial nuclear power facilities.

[e]The water sector includes drinking water and wastewater systems.

[f]The U.S. Coast Guard is the SSA for the maritime transportation mode within the transportation systems sector.

[g]In accordance with HSPD-7, the Department of Transportation and the Department of Homeland Security are to collaborate on all matters relating to transportation security and transportation infrastructure protection.

[h]As of October 2009, the Federal Protective Service had transitioned out of U.S. Immigration and Customs Enforcement to the National Protection and Programs Directorate.

[i]The Department of Education is the SSA for the education facilities subsector of the government facilities sector.

Appendix II: Objectives, Scope, and Methodology

To meet our first objective—determine the extent to which DHS has taken action to conduct security surveys and vulnerability assessments among high-priority CIKR—we reviewed DHS guidelines on the promotion and implementation of the security surveys and vulnerability assessments, records of outreach to CIKR stakeholders regarding these tools, and various DHS documents, including DHS's National Critical Infrastructure and Key Resources Protection Annual Report, on efforts to complete security surveys and vulnerability assessments. We also interviewed officials in the Protective Security Coordination Division, which is part of the Office of Infrastructure Protection (IP) in DHS's National Protection and Program Directorate, who are responsible for managing and administering DHS's security surveys and vulnerability assessments to learn about the actions they took to conduct these programs. We obtained and analyzed DHS data on the conduct of voluntary programs for fiscal years 2009 through 2011—which are maintained in DHS's Link Encrypted Network System (LENS) database and compared those records with the National Critical Infrastructure Prioritization Program (NCIPP) list of the high-priority CIKR assets—to determine the extent to which DHS performed security surveys and vulnerability assessments at high-priority assets.[1] To assess the reliability of the data, we reviewed existing documentation about the data systems and spoke with knowledgeable agency officials responsible for matching the two databases to discuss the results of our comparison and to learn about their efforts to match LENS data with the NCIPP lists. While the information in each database was sufficiently reliable for the purposes of providing a general overview of the program, issues with the comparability of information in each database exist, which are discussed in this report. To do our comparison, we used a Statistical Analysis System (SAS) program to match the different data sets and summarize the results. Because we found that assets in the LENS database and NCIPP lists did not share common formats or identifiers that allowed us to easily match them, we had to match the data based on asset names and addresses. However, names and addresses were generally not entered in a standardized way, so we had to develop a process to standardize the available information and identify potential matches based on similar names or addresses. In our attempt to match the data sets, we did the following:

---

[1] LENS is DHS's primary database for tracking efforts to promote and complete security surveys and assessments. NCIPP lists are used to prioritize assets that are subject to these programs.

GAO-12-378 Critical Infrastructure Protection

- Standardized the date formats for fields that tracked when assessments were conducted (dates across lists might have formats such as 01/01/10 or 1/1/2010 and needed to be standardized to ensure appropriate matching within certain time frames).
- Standardized the labels for sectors (across data sets, a sector might be listed as Chemical & Hazardous Materials Industry, Chemical and Hazardous Materials Indus, or 'Chemical').
- Standardized state fields (across data sets, a state might be listed as Alabama or AL).
- Identified exact matches between the data sets on the asset name and the state name.
- Identified potential matches between the data sets based on asset name, asset address, and state. Specifically, we used a SAS function (SPEDIS) that measures asymmetric spelling distance between words, to determine the likelihood that names and addresses from two data sets did match and to generate possible pairs of matching assets. The possible matches for an asset were written to a spreadsheet, which we reviewed to determine a potential match.

As noted in the report, the inconsistencies between the data sets prevented us from determining definitively the extent to which assets on one list were also present in the other list. For example, in some cases assets seemed to be potential matches but there were differences in the sector listed or inconsistent company names and addresses. Thus we report separately on assets that were exact matches based on asset name and those that were potential matches. We also examined the inconsistencies we found with respect to DHS's guidance on gathering data on participation in the security survey and vulnerability assessments and compared the findings to the criteria in *Standards for Internal Control in the Federal Government*.[2] We also compared the results of our

---

[2] GAO, *Standards for Internal Control in the Federal Government*, GAO/AIMD-00-21.3.1 (Washington, D.C.: November 1999). Internal control is an integral component of an organization's management that provides reasonable assurance that the following objectives are being achieved: effectiveness and efficiency of operations, reliability of financial reporting, and compliance with applicable laws and regulations. These standards, issued pursuant to the requirements of the Federal Managers' Financial Integrity Act of 1982 (FMFIA), provide the overall framework for establishing and maintaining internal control in the federal government. Also pursuant to FMFIA, the Office of Management and Budget issued Circular A-123, revised December 21, 2004, to provide the specific requirements for assessing the reporting on internal controls. Internal control standards and the definition of internal control in Circular A-123 are based on GAO's *Standards for Internal Control in the Federal Government*.

analyses with GAO reports on performance measurement, including ways
to use program data to measure results.[3]

In addition, to address the first objective, we also interviewed
representatives—asset owners and operators—at 10 selected assets,
also known as facilities, in 4 of the 18 sectors—the water, dams,
commercial facilities, and energy sectors—to discuss their views on DHS
efforts to work with asset owners and operators and conduct DHS's
voluntary security surveys and vulnerability assessments. We also
contacted industry association representatives from the 4 sectors to
discuss their views on DHS efforts to promote and conduct these
activities. We selected these asset and industry representatives to take
into account (1) sectors with a mix of regulations related to security; (2)
sectors where DHS's IP and non-DHS agencies are the SSAs—DHS for
the commercial facilities sector and dams sector, the Department of
Energy for the energy sector, and the Environmental Protection Agency
for the water sector; (3) sectors where security surveys and vulnerability
assessments had been conducted; and (4) geographic dispersion. We
selected three states—California, New Jersey, and Virginia—where,
based on our preliminary review of DHS's LENS database and the NCIPP
lists, security surveys and vulnerabilities assessments may have been
performed at high-priority assets. At these assets, we, among other
things, focused on the role of protective security advisors (PSA) who
serve as liaisons between DHS and security stakeholders, including asset
owners and operators, in local communities. We also reviewed PSA
program guidance and interviewed 4 of 88 PSAs—PSAs from California,
New Jersey and from the National Capital Region (encompassing
Washington, D.C., suburban Virginia, and suburban Maryland)—to
discuss the roles and responsibilities in partnering with asset owners and
operators and in promoting security surveys and vulnerability
assessments. While the results of our interviews cannot be generalized to
reflect the views of all asset owners and operators and PSAs nationwide,
the information obtained provided insights into DHS efforts to promote
participation in its security survey and vulnerability assessment programs.

---

[3] GAO, *Managing For Results: Assessing the Quality of Program Performance Data*,
GAO/GGD-00-140R (Washington, D.C.: May 25, 2000), and *Managing for Results:
Challenges in Producing Credible Performance Information*, GAO/T-GGD/RCED-00-134
(Washington, D.C.: Mar. 22, 2000).

We also conducted a survey of 83 of 88 PSAs, those who, based on lists
provided by DHS officials, had been in their positions for at least 1 year.
We conducted the survey to gather information on PSAs' efforts to
promote and implement security surveys and vulnerability assessments,
and identify challenges PSAs face when conducting these. GAO staff
familiar with the critical infrastructure protection subject matter designed
draft questionnaires in close collaboration with a social science survey
specialist. We conducted pretests with three PSAs to help further refine
our questions, develop new questions, clarify any ambiguous portions of
the survey, and identify any potentially biased questions. We launched
our web-based survey on October 3, 2011, and received all responses by
November 18, 2011. Log-in information for the web-based survey was e-
mailed to all participants. We sent one follow-up e-mail message to all
nonrespondents 2 weeks later and received responses from 80 out of 83
PSAs surveyed (96 percent).

Because the survey was conducted with all eligible PSAs, there are no
sampling errors. However, the practical difficulties of conducting any
survey may introduce nonsampling errors. For example, differences in
how a particular question is interpreted, the sources of information
available to respondents, or the types of people who do not respond can
introduce unwanted variability into the survey results. We included steps
in both the data collection and data analysis stages to minimize such
nonsampling errors. We collaborated with a GAO social science survey
specialist to design draft questionnaires, and versions of the
questionnaire were pretested with 3 PSAs. In addition, we provided a
draft of the questionnaire to DHS's IP for review and comment. From
these pretests and reviews, we made revisions as necessary. We
examined the survey results and performed computer analyses to identify
inconsistencies and other indications of error. A second independent
analyst checked the accuracy of all computer analyses.

Regarding our second objective—to determine the extent to which DHS
shared the results of security surveys and vulnerability assessments with
asset owners and operators and SSAs—we reviewed available DHS
guidelines and reports on efforts to share security survey and vulnerability
assessment results with stakeholders and compared DHS's sharing of
information with standards in the NIPP. We accessed, downloaded, and
analyzed LENS data for information regarding the asset owners and
operators that participated in DHS security surveys and vulnerability
assessments during fiscal years 2009 through 2011. To assess the
reliability of the data, we spoke with knowledgeable agency officials about
their quality assurance process. During the course of our review DHS

began taking action to clean up the data and address some of the data inconsistencies we discuss in this report. We found the data to be sufficiently reliable for providing a general overview of the program, but issues with the missing information in the LENS database exist and are discussed in this report. We compared the results of our analysis with DHS criteria regarding the timeliness of security surveys and vulnerability assessments, criteria in *Standards for Internal Control in the Federal Government*,[4] and the NIPP.[5]

We also used the LENS database, the NCIPP lists, and DHS documentation showing all assets that had received a security survey or a vulnerability assessment to select a nonrandom sample of high-priority assets from 4 sectors—the commercial facilities, dams, energy, and water sectors—and spoke with representatives from these selected assets to garner their opinions on the value of these voluntary programs and how they used the information DHS shared with them. In addition, we reviewed the 2009 and 2010 sector annual reports and the 2010 sector-specific plans for all CIKR sectors to assess if and how results of the security surveys and vulnerability assessments were included. We also interviewed SSA officials from our 4 selected sectors to learn what information DHS shared with them and how that information was used, and to discuss their overall relationship with DHS with respect to receiving and using data from DHS security surveys and vulnerability assessments. While the results of these interviews cannot be generalized to all SSAs, the results provided us with valuable insight into the dissemination and usefulness of information DHS provided from security surveys and vulnerability assessments. Furthermore, we interviewed DHS officials regarding their efforts to enhance the information they provide to SSAs from security surveys and vulnerability assessments.

With regard to our third objective—determine the extent to which DHS assessed the effectiveness of the security survey and vulnerability assessment programs, including any action needed to improve DHS's management of the programs—we reviewed DHS documents and our past reports,[6] and DHS Office of Inspector General (OIG) reports[7] on

---

[4] GAO/AIMD-00-21.3.1.

[5] See DHS, *National Infrastructure Protection Plan, Partnering to Enhance Protection and Resiliency* (Washington, D.C.: January 2009).

[6] See a list of related GAO products at the end of this report.

DHS efforts to assess the effectiveness of its programs. We interviewed DHS officials and reviewed DHS guidelines on procedures for following up with asset owners and operators that have participated in these programs and to discuss the results of DHS efforts to conduct these follow-ups. We also (1) examined DHS documents that discussed the results of DHS efforts to conduct follow-ups and (2) analyzed the instrument used to contact owners and operators, as well as the questions asked to assess its effectiveness. In addition, we analyzed available data on DHS efforts to perform follow-ups for the period from January 2011 through September 30, 2011, and compared DHS data with DHS guidelines that discussed the number of days DHS officials were to begin follow-ups after providing the results of security surveys and vulnerabilities to asset owners and operators. We also compared the results or our work with criteria in *Standards for Internal Control in the Federal Government*[8] and the NIPP,[9] particularly those related to performance measurement. Finally, we spoke to CIKR officials in our sample sectors to learn how DHS personnel in the field had followed up on security surveys and vulnerability assessments and whether asset owners and operators were making changes based on the results, and if not why.

We conducted this performance audit from June 2011 through May 2012 in accordance with generally accepted government auditing standards. Those standards require that we plan and perform the audit to obtain sufficient, appropriate evidence to provide a reasonable basis for our findings and conclusions based on our audit objectives. We believe that the evidence obtained provides a reasonable basis for our findings and conclusions based on our audit objectives.

---

[7] DHS OIG, *Planning, Management, and Systems Issues Hinder DHS' Efforts to Protect Cyberspace and the Nation's Cyber Infrastructure*, OIG-11-89 (Washington, D.C.: June 2011), and *Protective Security Advisor Program Efforts to Build Effective Critical Infrastructure Partnerships: Oil and Natural Gas Subsector*, OIG-11-12 (Washington, D.C.: November 2010).

[8] GAO/AIMD 00-21.3.1.

[9] See DHS, *National Infrastructure Protection Plan*.

Appendix III: Results of the Survey of Protective Security Advisors

This appendix provides information on our survey of Protective Security Advisors, which we used to gather information on efforts to promote and implement the voluntary programs offered by DHS and the challenges faced when conducting security surveys and vulnerability assessments. We conducted a Web-based survey of all 83 Protective Security Advisors who had been in their positions for at least one year. We received responses from 80, for a response rate of 96 percent. Our survey was composed of closed- and open-ended questions. In this appendix, we include all the survey questions and aggregate results of responses to the closed-ended questions; we do not provide information on responses provided to the open-ended questions. Percentages may not total to 100 due to rounding. For a more detailed discussion of our survey methodology, see appendix II.

Survey Respondent Information

1. Please provide the following information about the Protective Security Advisor responsible for completing this questionnaire.

Data intentionally not reported

Region:

Data intentionally not reported

District (if applicable):

Data intentionally not reported

Number of years as a PSA
(Round up to nearest year):

Mean	Median	Minimum	Maximum	Number of respondents
5.0	6	2	7	80

Training and Guidance

2. Did you receive the Enhanced Critical Infrastructure Protection (ECIP) Initiative Standard Operating Procedures (SOP) guidance dated February 2011?

Yes	No	Don't know	
%	%	%	Number of respondents
100.0	0.0	0.0	80

3. *(If yes to Q2)* How useful did you find the ECIP SOP guidance for **promoting** ECIPs?

Very useful	Moderately useful	Slightly useful	Not at all useful	Don't know	Number of respondents
%	%	%	%	%	
41.3	42.5	13.8	2.5	0.0	80

If you answered "slightly useful" or "not at all useful", please explain why:

Data intentionally not reported

4. *(If yes to Q2)* How useful did you find the ECIP SOP guidance for **conducting** ECIPs?

Very useful	Moderately useful	Slightly useful	Not at all useful	Don't know	Number of respondents
%	%	%	%	%	
43.8	43.8	8.8	1.3	2.5	80

If you answered "slightly useful" or "not at all useful", please explain why:

Data intentionally not reported

5. Did you receive training on the Enhanced Critical Infrastructure Protection (ECIP) **Initiative program**?

Yes	No	Don't know	Number of respondents
%	%	%	
97.5	2.5	0.0	80

6. *(If yes to Q5)* How useful did you find the ECIP training?

Very useful	Moderately useful	Slightly useful	Not at all useful	Don't know	Number of respondents
%	%	%	%	%	
61.0	35.1	2.6	1.3	0.0	77

If you answered "slightly useful" or "not at all useful", please explain why:

Data intentionally not reported

Usefulness of ECIPs

7. In your opinion, how useful is the ECIP **Initiative program** for reducing risk at CI facilities?

Very useful	Moderately useful	Slightly useful	Not at all useful	Don't know	Number of respondents
%	%	%	%	%	

| 58.8 | 30.0 | 10.0 | 0.0 | 1.3 | 80 |

Please explain your opinion about the usefulness of the ECIP Initiative program:

Data intentionally not reported

8. In your opinion, how useful is the ECIP **Infrastructure Survey Tool (IST)** for reducing risk at CI facilities?

Very useful	Moderately useful	Slightly useful	Not at all useful	Don't know	Number of respondents
%	%	%	%	%	
64.6	20.3	13.9	0.0	1.3	79

Please explain your opinion about the usefulness of the ECIP IST:

Data intentionally not reported

9. In your opinion, how useful is the ECIP **Facility Dashboard** for reducing risk at CI facilities?

Very useful	Moderately useful	Slightly useful	Not at all useful	Don't know	Number of respondents
%	%	%	%	%	
70.0	18.8	7.5	2.5	1.3	80

Please explain your opinion about the usefulness of the ECIP Facility Dashboard:

Data intentionally not reported

Participation in ECIP Site Visits

10. How often have you heard each of the following reasons from facilities who declined to participate in an ECIP **site visit**? (Select one answer in each row.)

a. The facility does not want to participate in additional facility assessments because it is already subject to Federal or State regulation/inspection.

Often	Sometimes	Rarely	Never	Don't know	Number of respondents
%	%	%	%	%	
16.3	38.8	27.5	15.0	2.5	80

b. The facility does not have time or resources to participate.

Often	Sometimes	Rarely	Never	Don't know	Number of respondents
%	%	%	%	%	
7.5	30.0	32.5	28.8	1.3	80

c. Facility owners and operators are not willing to sign Protected Critical Infrastructure Information Express statements due to legal concerns over the protection and dissemination of the data collected.

Often	Sometimes	Rarely	Never	Don't know	Number of respondents
%	%	%	%	%	
21.3	36.3	22.5	18.8	1.3	80

d. The entity that owns/oversees the facility declines to participate as a matter of policy.

Often	Sometimes	Rarely	Never	Don't know	Number of respondents
%	%	%	%	%	
12.5	32.5	27.5	23.8	3.8	80

e. Facility owners and operators have a diminished perception of threat against the facility.

Often	Sometimes	Rarely	Never	Don't know	Number of respondents
%	%	%	%	%	
6.3	21.3	33.8	36.3	2.5	80

f. The facility already received a risk assessment through a private company and participation in the voluntary assessment would be redundant or duplicative.

Often	Sometimes	Rarely	Never	Don't know	Number of respondents
%	%	%	%	%	
2.5	25.0	38.8	32.5	1.3	80

g. Identification of security gaps may render the owner of the facility liable for damages should an incident occur.

Often	Sometimes	Rarely	Never	Don't know	Number of respondents
%	%	%	%	%	
16.3	27.5	23.8	30.0	2.5	80

What other reasons, if any, have you heard for facilities declining ECIP site visits?

Data intentionally not reported

11. Have you found that higher priority facilities (Level 1 or 2) are more or less likely to participate in ECIP site visits than lower priority facilities?

Much more likely	Somewhat more likely	Equally likely	Somewhat less likely	Much less likely	Don't know	Number of respondents
%	%	%	%	%	%	
12.5	13.8	50.0	17.5	3.8	2.5	80

12. If you answered somewhat less likely or much less likely, what do you see as the reasons for the lower participation by the higher priority facilities?

Data intentionally not reported

13. What factors do you believe are important to facilities considering participating in an ECIP **site visit**?

Data intentionally not reported

Participation in ECIP IST

14. How often have you heard each of the following reasons from facilities who declined to participate in an ECIP **IST**?
(Select one answer in each row.)

a. The facility does not want to participate in additional facility assessments because it is already subject to Federal or State regulation/inspection.

Often	Sometimes	Rarely	Never	Don't know	Number of respondents
%	%	%	%	%	
16.5	36.7	32.9	12.7	1.3	79

b. The facility does not have time or resources to participate.

Often	Sometimes	Rarely	Never	Don't know	Number of respondents
%	%	%	%	%	
7.6	27.8	38.0	25.3	1.3	79

c. Facility owners and operators are not willing to sign Protected Critical Infrastructure Information Express statements due to legal concerns over the protection and dissemination of the data collected.

Often	Sometimes	Rarely	Never	Don't know	Number of respondents
%	%	%	%	%	
20.3	32.9	29.1	16.5	1.3	79

d. The entity that owns/oversees the facility declines to participate as a matter of policy.

Often	Sometimes	Rarely	Never	Don't know	Number of respondents
%	%	%	%	%	
10.4	32.5	32.5	23.4	1.3	77

e. Facility owners and operators have a diminished perception of threat against the facility.

Often	Sometimes	Rarely	Never	Don't know	Number of respondents
%	%	%	%	%	
3.8	27.8	31.6	34.2	2.5	79

f. The facility already received a risk assessment through a private company and participation in the voluntary assessment would be redundant or duplicative.

Often	Sometimes	Rarely	Never	Don't know	Number of respondents
%	%	%	%	%	
7.6	25.3	40.5	25.3	1.3	79

g. Identification of security gaps may render the owner of the facility liable for damages should an incident occur.

Often	Sometimes	Rarely	Never	Don't know	Number of respondents
%	%	%	%	%	
15.2	29.1	22.8	31.6	1.3	79

h. Facility's security program is not yet mature enough to benefit from participation.

Often	Sometimes	Rarely	Never	Don't know	Number of respondents
%	%	%	%	%	
1.3	7.7	30.8	57.7	2.6	78

What other reasons, if any, have you heard for facilities declining to participate in an ECIP IST?

Data intentionally not reported

15. Have you found that higher priority facilities (Level 1 or 2) are more or less likely to participate in ECIP ISTs than lower priority facilities?

Much more likely	Somewhat more likely	Equally likely	Somewhat less likely	Much less likely	Don't know	Number of respondents
%	%	%	%	%	%	
9.0	12.8	51.3	17.9	6.4	2.6	78

16. If you answered somewhat less likely or much less likely, what do you see as the reasons for the lower participation by the higher priority facilities?

Data intentionally not reported

17. How much of an incentive do you believe each of the following are for encouraging participation in an ECIP IST?
(Select one answer in each row.)

a. Access to subject matter expertise

Great incentive	Moderate incentive	Slight incentive	No incentive	Don't know	Number of respondents
%	%	%	%	%	
45.6	35.4	15.2	3.8	0.0	79

b. Timely and actionable vulnerability information

Great incentive	Moderate incentive	Slight incentive	No incentive	Don't know	Number of respondents
%	%	%	%	%	
41.8	39.2	13.9	5.1	0.0	79

c. Ability to compare facility to sector Protective Measures Index

Great incentive	Moderate incentive	Slight incentive	No incentive	Don't know	Number of respondents
%	%	%	%	%	
58.2	36.7	5.1	0.0	0.0	79

d. Appeal to public service (patriotic duty)

Great incentive	Moderate incentive	Slight incentive	No incentive	Don't know	Number of respondents
%	%	%	%	%	
10.1	27.8	41.8	19.0	1.3	79

e. Opportunity to improve facility security using a free government service

Great incentive	Moderate incentive	Slight incentive	No incentive	Don't know	Number of respondents
%	%	%	%	%	
65.8	27.8	5.1	1.3	0.0	79

What other incentives, if any, do you believe would encourage participation?

Data intentionally not reported

18. Are there any actions the Office of Infrastructure Protection could take that you believe could enhance participation in ECIP ISTs?

Data intentionally not reported

Effectiveness of ECIP Program

19. In your opinion, how effective is the voluntary ECIP **Initiative program** in reducing risk for each of the following sectors (if applicable to your district)?
(Select one answer in each row.)

a. Agriculture and Food

Very effective	Moderately effective	Slightly effective	Not at all effective	Not applicable	Number of respondents
%	%	%	%	%	
26.0	27.3	32.5	7.8	6.5	77

b. Defense Industrial Base

Very effective	Moderately effective	Slightly effective	Not at all effective	Not applicable	Number of respondents
%	%	%	%	%	
19.0	30.4	29.1	11.4	10.1	79

c. Energy

Very effective	Moderately effective	Slightly effective	Not at all effective	Not applicable	Number of respondents
%	%	%	%	%	
42.1	28.9	23.7	3.9	1.3	76

d. Healthcare and Public Health

Very effective	Moderately effective	Slightly effective	Not at all effective	Not applicable	Number of respondents
%	%	%	%	%	
49.4	31.6	15.2	1.3	2.5	79

e. National Monuments and Icons

Very effective	Moderately effective	Slightly effective	Not at all effective	Not applicable	Number of respondents
%	%	%	%	%	
24.1	27.8	25.3	5.1	17.7	79

f. Banking and Finance

Very effective	Moderately effective	Slightly effective	Not at all effective	Not applicable	Number of respondents
%	%	%	%	%	
31.2	35.1	18.2	6.5	9.1	77

g. Water

Very effective	Moderately effective	Slightly effective	Not at all effective	Not applicable	Number of respondents
%	%	%	%	%	
62.5	21.3	12.5	0.0	3.8	80

h. Chemical

Very effective	Moderately effective	Slightly effective	Not at all effective	Not applicable	Number of respondents
%	%	%	%	%	
30.0	16.3	18.8	2.5	32.5	80

i. Commercial Facilities

Very effective	Moderately effective	Slightly effective	Not at all effective	Not applicable	Number of respondents
%	%	%	%	%	
63.8	26.3	8.8	0.0	1.3	80

j. Critical Manufacturing

Very effective	Moderately effective	Slightly effective	Not at all effective	Not applicable	Number of respondents
%	%	%	%	%	
36.3	27.5	18.8	3.8	13.8	80

k. Dams

Very effective	Moderately effective	Slightly effective	Not at all effective	Not applicable	Number of respondents
%	%	%	%	%	
39.2	27.8	20.3	5.1	7.6	79

l. Emergency Services

Very effective	Moderately effective	Slightly effective	Not at all effective	Not applicable	Number of respondents
%	%	%	%	%	
33.8	35.0	25.0	1.3	5.0	80

m. Nuclear Reactors, Materials, and Waste

Very effective	Moderately effective	Slightly effective	Not at all effective	Not applicable	Number of respondents
%	%	%	%	%	
22.5	18.8	22.5	13.8	22.5	80

n. Information Technology

Very effective	Moderately effective	Slightly effective	Not at all effective	Not applicable	Number of respondents
%	%	%	%	%	
25.0	33.8	26.3	5.0	10.0	80

o. Communications

Very effective	Moderately effective	Slightly effective	Not at all effective	Not applicable	Number of respondents
%	%	%	%	%	
27.8	38.0	19.0	3.8	11.4	79

p. Postal and Shipping

Very effective	Moderately effective	Slightly effective	Not at all effective	Not applicable	Number of respondents
%	%	%	%	%	
29.9	32.5	22.1	5.2	10.4	77

q. Transportation Systems

Very effective	Moderately effective	Slightly effective	Not at all effective	Not applicable	Number of respondents
%	%	%	%	%	
45.0	31.3	20.0	1.3	2.5	80

r. Government Facilities

Very effective	Moderately effective	Slightly effective	Not at all effective	Not applicable	Number of respondents
%	%	%	%	%	
54.4	22.8	15.2	1.3	6.3	79

If you responded not applicable to any of the sectors above, please explain.

Data intentionally not reported

20. Are you aware of any factors that drive differing levels of participation in the voluntary ECIP Initiative program by sector? Please explain.

Data intentionally not reported

SAVs

21. In your opinion, how useful are **SAVs** as a tool for reducing risk at CI facilities?

Very useful	Moderately useful	Slightly useful	Not at all useful	Don't know	Number of respondents
%	%	%	%	%	
56.4	28.2	11.5	2.6	1.3	78

Please explain your opinion about the usefulness of SAVs:

Data intentionally not reported

22. How often have you heard each of the following reasons from facilities who declined to participate in a **SAV**?
(Select one answer in each row.)

a. The facility does not want to participate in additional facility assessments because it is already subject to Federal or State regulation/inspection.

Often	Sometimes	Rarely	Never	Don't know	Number of respondents
%	%	%	%	%	
10.0	35.0	36.3	16.3	2.5	80

b. The facility does not have time or resources to participate.

Often	Sometimes	Rarely	Never	Don't know	Number of respondents
%	%	%	%	%	
7.6	32.9	36.7	20.3	2.5	79

c. Facility owners and operators are not willing to sign Protected Critical Infrastructure Information Express statements due to legal concerns over the protection and dissemination of the data collected.

Often	Sometimes	Rarely	Never	Don't know	Number of respondents
%	%	%	%	%	
10.0	32.5	33.8	21.3	2.5	80

d. The entity that owns/oversees the facility declines to participate as a matter of policy.

Often	Sometimes	Rarely	Never	Don't know	Number of respondents
%	%	%	%	%	
10.0	27.5	35.0	25.0	2.5	80

e. Facility owners and operators have a diminished perception of threat against the facility.

Often	Sometimes	Rarely	Never	Don't know	Number of respondents
%	%	%	%	%	
5.1	16.5	38.0	36.7	3.8	79

f. The facility already received a risk assessment through a private company and participation in the voluntary assessment would be redundant or duplicative.

Often	Sometimes	Rarely	Never	Don't know	Number of respondents
%	%	%	%	%	
5.0	26.3	38.8	27.5	2.5	80

g. Identification of security gaps may render the owner of the facility liable for damages should an incident occur.

Often	Sometimes	Rarely	Never	Don't know	Number of respondents
%	%	%	%	%	
11.3	30.0	28.8	26.3	3.8	80

h. Facility's security program is not yet mature enough to benefit from participation.

Often	Sometimes	Rarely	Never	Don't know	Number of respondents
%	%	%	%	%	
1.3	7.5	35.0	52.5	3.8	80

What other reasons, if any, have you heard for facilities declining to participate in a SAV?

Data intentionally not reported

23. Have you found that higher priority facilities (Level 1 or 2) are more or less likely to participate in SAVs than lower priority facilities?

Much more likely	Somewhat more likely	Equally likely	Somewhat less likely	Much less likely	Don't know	Number of respondents
%	%	%	%	%	%	
8.9	13.9	50.6	13.9	5.1	7.6	79

24. If you answered somewhat less likely or much less likely, what do you see as the reasons for the lower participation by the higher priority facilities?

Data intentionally not reported

25. How much of an incentive do you believe each of the following are for encouraging participation in a SAV?
(Select one answer in each row.)

a. Access to subject matter expertise

Great incentive	Moderate incentive	Slight incentive	No incentive	Don't know	Number of respondents
%	%	%	%	%	
53.2	32.9	8.9	2.5	2.5	79

b. Timely and actionable vulnerability information

Great incentive	Moderate incentive	Slight incentive	No incentive	Don't know	Number of respondents
%	%	%	%	%	
45.6	35.4	13.9	2.5	2.5	79

c. Ability to compare facility to sector Protective Measures Index

Great incentive	Moderate incentive	Slight incentive	No incentive	Don't know	Number of respondents
%	%	%	%	%	
50.6	30.4	12.7	1.3	5.1	79

d. Appeal to public service (patriotic duty)

Great incentive	Moderate incentive	Slight incentive	No incentive	Don't know	Number of respondents
%	%	%	%	%	
12.7	13.9	45.6	22.8	5.1	79

e. Opportunity to improve facility security using a free government service

Great incentive	Moderate incentive	Slight incentive	No incentive	Don't know	Number of respondents
%	%	%	%	%	
69.6	22.8	5.1	0.0	2.5	79

What other incentives, if any, do you believe would encourage participation?

Data intentionally not reported

26. Are there any actions the Office of Infrastructure Protection could take that you believe could enhance participation in SAVs?

Data intentionally not reported

Effectiveness of SAVs

27. In your opinion, how effective is the voluntary **SAV program** in reducing risk for each of the following sectors (if applicable to your district)?
(Select one answer in each row.)

a. Agriculture and Food

Very effective	Moderately effective	Slightly effective	Not at all effective	Not applicable	Number of respondents
%	%	%	%	%	
26.9	28.2	21.8	7.7	15.4	78

b. Defense Industrial Base

Very effective	Moderately effective	Slightly effective	Not at all effective	Not applicable	Number of respondents
%	%	%	%	%	
20.5	32.1	23.1	6.4	17.9	78

c. Energy

Very effective	Moderately effective	Slightly effective	Not at all effective	Not applicable	Number of respondents
%	%	%	%	%	
51.9	19.0	22.8	1.3	5.1	79

d. Healthcare and Public Health

Very effective	Moderately effective	Slightly effective	Not at all effective	Not applicable	Number of respondents
%	%	%	%	%	
49.4	25.3	15.2	1.3	8.9	79

e. National Monuments and Icons

Very effective	Moderately effective	Slightly effective	Not at all effective	Not applicable	Number of respondents
%	%	%	%	%	
29.5	24.4	23.1	2.6	20.5	78

f. Banking and Finance

Very effective	Moderately effective	Slightly effective	Not at all effective	Not applicable	Number of respondents
%	%	%	%	%	
38.5	32.1	17.9	2.6	9.0	78

g. Water

Very effective	Moderately effective	Slightly effective	Not at all effective	Not applicable	Number of respondents
%	%	%	%	%	
61.5	19.2	9.0	2.6	7.7	78

h. Chemical

Very effective	Moderately effective	Slightly effective	Not at all effective	Not applicable	Number of respondents
%	%	%	%	%	
35.4	16.5	13.9	1.3	32.9	79

i. Commercial Facilities

Very effective	Moderately effective	Slightly effective	Not at all effective	Not applicable	Number of respondents
%	%	%	%	%	
59.0	26.9	10.3	0.0	3.8	78

j. Critical Manufacturing

Very effective	Moderately effective	Slightly effective	Not at all effective	Not applicable	Number of respondents
%	%	%	%	%	
41.0	24.4	15.4	1.3	17.9	78

k. Dams

Very effective	Moderately effective	Slightly effective	Not at all effective	Not applicable	Number of respondents
%	%	%	%	%	
41.8	25.3	16.5	5.1	11.4	79

l. Emergency Services

Very effective	Moderately effective	Slightly effective	Not at all effective	Not applicable	Number of respondents
%	%	%	%	%	
34.2	36.7	19.0	1.3	8.9	79

m. Nuclear Reactors, Materials, and Waste

Very effective	Moderately effective	Slightly effective	Not at all effective	Not applicable	Number of respondents
%	%	%	%	%	
24.1	11.4	25.3	10.1	29.1	79

n. Information Technology

Very effective	Moderately effective	Slightly effective	Not at all effective	Not applicable	Number of respondents
%	%	%	%	%	
32.9	27.8	21.5	3.8	13.9	79

o. Communications

Very effective	Moderately effective	Slightly effective	Not at all effective	Not applicable	Number of respondents
%	%	%	%	%	
34.2	30.4	19.0	2.5	13.9	79

p. Postal and Shipping

Very effective	Moderately effective	Slightly effective	Not at all effective	Not applicable	Number of respondents
%	%	%	%	%	
30.4	27.8	20.3	2.5	19.0	79

q. Transportation Systems

Very effective	Moderately effective	Slightly effective	Not at all effective	Not applicable	Number of respondents
%	%	%	%	%	
51.9	24.1	15.2	1.3	7.6	79

GAO-12-378 Critical Infrastructure Protection

r. Government Facilities

Very effective	Moderately effective	Slightly effective	Not at all effective	Not applicable	Number of respondents
%	%	%	%	%	
52.6	25.6	11.5	1.3	9.0	78

If you responded not applicable to any of the sectors above, please explain.

Data intentionally not reported

28. Are you aware of any factors that drive differing levels of participation in the voluntary SAV program by sector? Please explain.

Data intentionally not reported

Challenges

29. What challenges, if any, do you face when implementing voluntary CI protection programs associated with ECIPs and SAVs?

Data intentionally not reported

Submitting and Printing the Survey

30. Are you ready to submit your final completed survey to GAO?
(This is equivalent to mailing a completed paper survey to us. It tells us that your answers are official and final.)

Yes, my survey is complete - To submit your final responses, please click on "Exit" below"	No, my survey is not yet complete - To save your responses for later, please click on "Exit" below"	Number of respondents
%	%	
100.0	0.0	80

You may view and print your completed survey by clicking on the Summary link in the menu to the left.

Appendix IV: Comments from the Department of Homeland Security

U.S. Department of Homeland Security
Washington, DC 20528

May 17, 2012

Mr. Stephen L. Caldwell
Director, Homeland Security & Justice Issues
U.S. Government Accountability Office
441 G Street, NW
Washington, DC 20548

Re: Draft Report GAO 12-378, "CRITICAL INFRASTRUCTURE PROTECTION: DHS
Could Better Manage Security Surveys and Vulnerability Assessments"

Dear Mr. Caldwell:

Thank you for the opportunity to review and comment on this draft report. The U.S. Department
of Homeland Security (DHS) appreciates the U.S. Government Accountability Office's (GAO's)
work in planning and conducting its review and issuing this report.

The Department was pleased to note the report's description of the National Protection and
Programs Directorate/Office of Infrastructure Protection's (NPPD/IP's) accomplishments and
activities undertaken to conduct voluntary security surveys and vulnerability assessments,
provide information to private-sector partners, and assess the effectiveness of security surveys
and vulnerability assessments. The report focused on Site Assistance Visit (SAV) vulnerability
assessments and Enhanced Critical Infrastructure Protection (ECIP) security surveys. NPPD/IP,
however, also conducts other assessment activities, including Buffer Zone Plans (BZPs) created
as part of the Buffer Zone Protection Program (BZPP). BZPs are considered vulnerability
assessments and are included as such within the *2008–2013 IP Strategic Plan*. In addition to
activities described during the time period covered by this report (Fiscal Years [FYs] 2009–
2011), NPPD/IP conducted 443 BZPs, 98 percent (435) of which were associated with
prioritized critical infrastructure facilities.

The Department concurs with all seven recommendations in the draft report. Specifically, GAO
recommended that the Assistant Secretary for Infrastructure Protection:

Recommendation 1: Develop plans with milestones and timeframes to resolve issues associated
with data inconsistencies and matching data on the list of high priority assets with data used to
track the conduct of security surveys and vulnerability assessments.

Response: Concur. NPPD/IP addressed this issue in 2011 with the assignment of unique
numerical identifiers to each asset in the Linking Encrypted Network System (LENS) assessment
database and the National Critical Infrastructure Prioritization Program (NCIPP) lists. As noted

in the report, the unique numerical identifiers are now used in the maintenance of current and future lists (FYs 2011 and FY 2012) to expediently generate a more accurate matched list of sites visited. It is now possible to cross-reference the NCIPP entries against the LENS assessment databases to more accurately and consistently report requested information, such as the number of visits or visit dates. Additional NCIPP quality assurance processes have been implemented to better verify individual asset data, such as geographic coordinates, street addresses, and facility names.

NPPD/IP's Homeland Infrastructure Threat and Risk Analysis Center (HITRAC), responsible for developing and maintaining the list of high priority assets, continues to collaborate with other NPPD/IP Divisions, Argonne National Laboratory (ANL), and other DHS partners to streamline and better organize the NCIPP, reporting periods, and data associated with assessments, surveys, and other NPPD/IP field activities.

Recommendation 2: Institutionalize realistic performance goals for appropriate levels of participation in security surveys and vulnerability assessments by high priority assets to measure how well DHS is achieving its goals.

Response: Concur. NPPD/IP continues its efforts to develop and implement performance measures relating to the completion of security surveys and vulnerability assessments for high-priority critical infrastructure assets. The FY 2012 Project Management Plans for the Protective Security Advisor (PSA) and Vulnerability Assessments Projects established realistic goals concerning the total number of assessments to be conducted and the proportion of the aforementioned facilities implementing improvements based on those assessments.

As NPPD/IP continues to refine and develop new goals and metrics to measure performance, the participation of high-priority assets continues to be an area of particular concentration. However, as the report noted, DHS critical infrastructure protection activities have expanded beyond individual Level 1 and Level 2 assets to focus on critical clusters and systems comprising a variety of assets. Many of the individual assets within a defined cluster or system are not themselves considered nationally significant (i.e., Level 1 and Level 2). This approach is in consonance with the DHS shift towards critical infrastructure resilience, which recognizes the importance of those non-Leveled assets and systems supporting Level 1 and Level 2 assets, other critical infrastructures, and communities as a whole. The concept of resilience understands that though an individual Level 1 or Level 2 facility may itself be highly secure, without the supporting operations of other less nationally significant assets and systems, the facility will fail. In recognition of this shift in emphasis, metrics, and goals intended to measure the participation of high-priority assets in vulnerability assessments and surveys may not be a strong or accurate indicator of the degree to which DHS is achieving its infrastructure protection and resilience goals.

In addition, any metric or goal developed to measure participation of high-priority assets must recognize and be understood within the context of the various factors that influence whether asset owners and operators participate. As the report noted, these include the voluntary nature of participation; the fact that successful outreach and participation in DHS infrastructure activity is

2

not measured solely by assessment participation; regulated status of certain facilities (e.g., Chemical Facilities Anti-Terrorism Standards facilities, nuclear reactors) that limits NPPD/IP's ability to conduct assessments and surveys; and the increased emphasis on regional activities such as RRAPs that are not necessarily focused on individual high-priority assets.

Finally, it is important to highlight that assessment goals are often impacted by emerging real-world threats that shift the focus of programmatic activities and Department priorities. This has occurred on numerous occasions such as the 2009 Najibullah Zazi case, the 2010 Improvised Explosive Devices Air Cargo threat, and current outreach to the American Jewish Community.

Recommendation 3: Design and implement a mechanism for systematically assessing why owners and operators of high priority assets decline to participate and develop a roadmap, with timeframes and milestones, for completing this effort.

Response: Concur. A mechanism for reporting this information is outlined in the ECIP Initiative Standard Operating Procedure (SOP); however NPPD/IP recognizes that additional clarification and guidance is needed to ensure effective implementation. NPPD/IP will review the SOP to accomplish the following: 1) determine if revisions to the existing process are required; and 2) develop supplementary guidance to aid PSAs in executing the process. NPPD/IP will initiate this review in the fourth quarter of FY 2012, after which time it will develop additional milestones for mechanism improvement. Recognizing that PSAs cannot compel an asset owner and operator to provide this information and that overly intrusive requests may damage the voluntary partnership between the owner and operator and DHS, data regarding facility abstention will be collected and reviewed to the greatest extent possible.

Recommendation 4: Develop timeframes and specific milestones for managing its efforts to improve the timely delivery of the results of security surveys and vulnerability assessments to asset owners and operators.

Response: Concur. As noted in the report, several factors impacting the delivery of security survey and vulnerability assessment reports within the timeframe of investigation have since been addressed. Specifically, the principal issues contributing to the SAV backlog (change of contractor, enhancements to the SAV tool, and changes to the data quality assurance process) have been resolved. The SAV backlog was eliminated in late January 2012.

In addition, it should be noted that NPPD/IP's plan to transition to a Web-based dashboard system will help mitigate the issue of timely report delivery. Eliminating the need for in-person delivery of the dashboard product ensures that delivery will not be dependent upon coordinated PSA and stakeholder schedules. Final dashboards will be considered as delivered when they are posted to the Web portal and thus made available to the facility owner and operator. Mechanisms will be built into the system to automatically notify owners and operators and NPPD/IP personnel when the dashboards are available.

NPPD/IP will continue to work with internal and external partners to ensure the accurate reporting and timely delivery of products to our customers and key stakeholders. In an effort to

3

improve timeliness, NPPD/IP is working with contractors and program staff to advance the processes and protocols governing the delivery of assessment and survey products to facilities. NPPD/IP has commenced a review of those assessments lacking a delivery date in LENS and is working with the PSAs to populate the missing information. An automatic notification is also being built into LENS to remind PSAs of their obligation to submit delivery date data.

Recommendation 5: Revise its plans to include when and how SSAs will be engaged in designing, testing, and implementing DHS's Web-based tool to address and mitigate any SSA concerns that may arise before the tool is finalized.

Response: Concur. As the primary consumers of the NPPD/IP assessment dashboards are individual facility owners and operators, associated tools and products have been developed to meet their specific needs. State and local homeland security officials are a second primary consumer of the assessments. Though SSAs are not the primary consumers of NPPD/IP assessments or assessment data, NPPD/IP will continue to engage with SSA representatives to obtain feedback regarding their preferred assessment data presentation. This engagement with the SSAs most importantly took place during the development of the critical sector-specific weights associated with the various security factors built into the assessment tool. The Web-based dashboard tool designed for asset owners and operators will be released to 18 PSAs for testing in May 2012, but is not expected to be widely available until January 2013. This initial pilot will consist only of those dashboards designed for individual owners and operators. Subsequent development of a state-level view (i.e., dashboard) of assessment data is anticipated following the successful deployment of the Web-based owner and operator dashboards. The elicitation of state and local dashboard requirements is ongoing via the State, Local, Tribal, Territorial Government Coordinating Council (SLTTGCC) and the NPPD/IP Regionalization Initiative. The concept for a sector-level view of assessment data has been proposed, and the requirements and feasibility of such a dashboard will be explored more fully following the completion of the state-level Web-based dashboard; NPPD/IP will engage the SSAs to determine any associated requirements.

Recommendation 6: Develop a roadmap with timeframes and specific milestones for reviewing the information it gathers from asset owners and operators to determine if follow-up visits should remain at 180 days for security surveys, and whether additional follow-ups are appropriate at intervals beyond the follow-ups initially performed.

Response: Concur. Post-assessment PSA follow-up visits fall at the 365 day mark for SAVs and the 180 day mark for ECIP security surveys. The timing of these follow-ups was determined as a means to begin collecting data on security improvements made in response to NPPD/IP surveys and assessments. Given that the updated SAV and associated 365 day follow-up process went into effect in January 2011, the first follow-up evaluations have only recently commenced. Prior to realigning the current SAV and ECIP follow-up intervals, NPPD/IP will collect, at minimum, 1 year of SAV follow-up data. Although NPPD/IP agrees that the 180-day period may not provide sufficient time for the implementation of security improvements (and has found the owner and operator feedback contained in the GAO report most informative in this regard), a change in follow-up procedure without a full year of comparative data would be premature.

4

NPPD/IP will analyze and compare the SAV 365-day and ECIP 180-day follow-up results in early calendar year 2013. Subsequent to this review, NPPD/IP will determine whether modifications to the follow-up intervals are required.

Recommendation 7: Consider the feasibility of expanding the follow-up program to gather and act upon data, as appropriate, on (1) security enhancements that are ongoing and planned that are attributable to DHS security surveys and vulnerability assessments and (2) factors, such as cost and perceptions of threat, that influence asset owner and operators decisions to make, or not make, enhancements based on the results of DHS security survey and assessments.

Response: Concur. Current follow-up questions do collect information regarding ongoing or planned security enhancements. NPPD/IP will continue to work with ANL and field deployed personnel to determine the best method for collecting information related to those factors influencing an asset's decision to implement or not implement a new protective measure or security enhancement.

Again, thank you for the opportunity to review and comment on this draft report. Technical comments were previously provided under separate cover. Please feel free to contact me if you have any questions. We look forward to working with you on future Homeland Security issues.

Sincerely,

Jim H. Crumpacker
Director
Departmental GAO-OIG Liaison Office

5

Appendix V: GAO Contact and Staff Acknowledgments

GAO Contact	Stephen L. Caldwell, (202) 512-8777 or CaldwellS@gao.gov
Staff Acknowledgments	In addition to the contact named above, John F. Mortin, Assistant Director, and Anthony DeFrank, Analyst-in-Charge, managed this assignment. Andrew M. Curry, Katherine M. Davis, Michele C. Fejfar, Lisa L. Fisher, Mitchell B. Karpman, Thomas F. Lombardi, and Mona E. Nichols-Blake made significant contributions to the work.

Related GAO Products

Critical Infrastructure Protection: DHS Has Taken Action Designed to Identify and Address Overlaps and Gaps in Critical Infrastructure Security Activities. GAO-11-537R. Washington, D.C.: May 19, 2011.

Critical Infrastructure Protection: DHS Efforts to Assess and Promote Resiliency Are Evolving but Program Management Could Be Strengthened. GAO-10-772. Washington, D.C.: September 23, 2010.

Critical Infrastructure Protection: Update to National Infrastructure Protection Plan Includes Increased Emphasis on Risk Management and Resilience. GAO-10-296. Washington, D.C.: March 5, 2010.

The Department of Homeland Security's (DHS) Critical Infrastructure Protection Cost-Benefit Report. GAO-09-654R. Washington, D.C.: June 26, 2009.

Information Technology: Federal Laws, Regulations, and Mandatory Standards to Securing Private Sector Information Technology Systems and Data in Critical Infrastructure Sectors. GAO-08-1075R. Washington, D.C.: September 16, 2008.

Risk Management: Strengthening the Use of Risk Management Principles in Homeland Security. GAO-08-904T. Washington, D.C.: June 25, 2008.

Critical Infrastructure: Sector Plans Complete and Sector Councils Evolving. GAO-07-1075T. Washington, D.C.: July 12, 2007.

Critical Infrastructure Protection: Sector Plans and Sector Councils Continue to Evolve. GAO-07-706R. Washington, D.C.: July 10, 2007.

Critical Infrastructure: Challenges Remain in Protecting Key Sectors. GAO-07-626T. Washington, D.C.: March 20, 2007.

Homeland Security: Progress Has Been Made to Address the Vulnerabilities Exposed by 9/11, but Continued Federal Action Is Needed to Further Mitigate Security Risks. GAO-07-375. Washington, D.C.: January 24, 2007.

Critical Infrastructure Protection: Progress Coordinating Government and Private Sector Efforts Varies by Sectors' Characteristics. GAO-07-39. Washington, D.C.: October 16, 2006.

Information Sharing: DHS Should Take Steps to Encourage More Widespread Use of Its Program to Protect and Share Critical Infrastructure Information. GAO-06-383. Washington, D.C.: April 17, 2006.

Risk Management: Further Refinements Needed to Assess Risks and Prioritize Protective Measures at Ports and Other Critical Infrastructure. GAO-06-91. Washington, D.C.: December 15, 2005.

Protection of Chemical and Water Infrastructure: Federal Requirements, Actions of Selected Facilities, and Remaining Challenges. GAO-05-327. Washington, D.C.: March 28, 2005.

Homeland Security: Agency Plans, Implementation, and Challenges Regarding the National Strategy for Homeland Security. GAO-05-33. Washington, D.C.: January 14, 2005.

Please Print on Recycled Paper.

51334712R00050

Made in the USA
Charleston, SC
19 January 2016